Blue-Collar Christianity

OTHER BOOKS BY RICHARD EXLEY

Perils of Power

The Rhythm of Life

The Painted Parable

The Other God —
Seeing God as He Really Is

Blue-Collar Christianity

by

RICHARD EXLEY

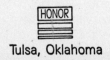

Tulsa, Oklahoma

Cover photo: Scott Miller

Blue-Collar Christianity
ISBN 0-89274-486-3
Copyright © 1989 by Richard Exley
7807 E. 76th St.
Tulsa, Oklahoma 74133-3648

Published by Honor Books
A Division of Harrison House, Inc.
P. O. Box 35035
Tulsa, Oklahoma 74153

DEDICATION

To Jack Ingram,
a "blue-collar" Christian
in his own right,
and a true friend
who celebrates my small successes
as if they were his own.

CONTENTS

Blue-Collar Christianity

ACKNOWLEDGMENTS

The completion of a book, any book, regardless of how insignificant the volume, is a team effort. The author may be the principal creator, but he does not labor alone.

In my case, I am indebted, in some way, to almost everyone I know. In particular to four congregations — the Assembly of God in Holly, Colorado; the First Assembly of God in Florence, Colorado; The Church of the Comforter in Craig, Colorado; and Christian Chapel in Tulsa, Oklahoma. I will always be grateful for the opportunity they afforded me to learn "blue-collar Christianity" firsthand. And for the patience they extended to me in my fumbling efforts to become a man of God and a minister.

I am particularly indebted to Mr. Keith Provance, General Manager of Harrison House Publishers. Not only is he a publisher with vision, but a very special friend. Writing, for the most part, is a solitary task, a lonely chore. That's as it should be; still, fortunate indeed is the writer who has a friend with whom he can share his work. Keith is such a friend, and his suggestions and encouragement have proven invaluable.

Years ago, almost twenty now, when becoming a writer was just a secret dream, I read *Journal Of A Novel* by John Steinbeck. While writing *East of Eden*, Steinbeck began each day's work with a letter to Pascal Covici, his friend and editor. These letters served to "warm him up" for the task at hand, and became a kind of commentary on the novel itself. Anyway, I can distinctly remember hoping that someday I might have a relationship like that. Now I do.

Of course, any acknowledgment would be incomplete without an expression of love and gratitude to Brenda, my wife of twenty-two years. She has remained a constant support, encouraging me in every way, and is the co-author of my most important work — life.

INTRODUCTION

In our house, Christianity wasn't a moral code, church membership or a way of behaving in public. It was a lifestyle — love with its sleeves rolled up! If there was a job to do, we did it. If there was a need, we did our best to meet it. Pleasing God and serving others was our highest goal.

Once when I was still in elementary school, we came out of church after prayer meeting on a Wednesday night and saw a transient family in a beat-up old car parked in front of the church. They looked tired, and a hungry baby whimpered from the broken-down back seat. Even as a child, I could see the hollow look in their eyes, the quiet desperation that had prematurely aged their faces, leaving them flat and empty. They were good people, just down on their luck, and too proud to ask for help. Still, it was obvious that they were hoping some of the Lord's people would have compassion on them.

Dad did. He walked right over to the driver's side of the car, stuck out his hand and introduced himself. He invited those people home for supper, although it was long past supper time, and told them they could spend the night with us.

We didn't have much ourselves, as I recall, but my folks were always more than willing to share what little we had, and soon the kitchen was full of friendly smells. Mother put together a simple meal of homemade bread, fried potatoes and ham. I followed Dad down into the half-finished basement where we collected two quarts of home-canned peaches for dessert. As we ascended the stairs, I distinctly remember the sound of ham sizzling in the skillet. Since that night it's always sounded like love to me, a good sound, friendly and comforting.

Another time Dad remodeled a small house for a young widow and her two children. Her husband, Merl, had died suddenly of a brain tumor, leaving her with almost nothing. Following the funeral, she was forced to move into more affordable housing and the only thing she could find was a small house which was desperately in need of repair.

When Dad learned about her situation, he offered to help. Night after night, for several weeks, we two boys and Mom accompanied him as he replaced the plumbing, put in new wiring, built cupboards for the kitchen and repainted inside and out. Finally, he was finished and that young mother and her two children had a small but comfortable place to call home. More than that, they knew they were not alone, that God had not forgotten them! That too is love.

Mom's a "blue-collar Christian" too in her own right. As an infant, she was adopted by a childless couple who were well past middle age. By the time I came along, Grandpa was in poor health and seldom left his home. Neither he nor Grandma could read or write and they existed on a small pension check. Naturally, Mother was their primary source of assistance, and she looked after them with loving kindness.

Their old-age pension checks came once a month, and when they did, Mother would take Grandma to town to do her monthly shopping. Sometimes I had to stay with Grandpa, if he wasn't feeling well. But more often than not, I was included in this monthly trek to town. I can't remember everything we did; in fact, almost all of the mundane details are lost to my memory. But I do remember that our shopping-day ritual included going to White's Bakery for glazed donuts and coffee.

Thinking about it now, I remember the delicious smell of fresh bread and all kinds of pastries, plus the obvious bond of love between my mother and her mother. It was as tangible as the smells pouring out of the kitchen and just as inviting. That kind of love is "blue-collar Christianity" at its best!

Mom loved Dad and us kids like that too, and there wasn't anything she wouldn't do for us. That's not to say that she had no identity of her own, only that providing a home for us was what she valued above all else. In fact, Joyce Coloney's description of her mother reminds me of my own: "My mother, born early in this century, took strength from her position as a homemaker. This is the work she chose to do in life — not being an executive secretary, for which she had been trained. Arranging my father's comforts and supervising and teaching us children was for her an honorable and productive goal."[1]

Like her, my mother would have been delighted to devote herself entirely to the task of homemaking, but she was unable to. When things got tight, she took in ironing in order to help make ends meet. Later, she began baby-sitting in our home. Both jobs were exhausting. In fact, either one alone would have been more than most women would have wanted to tackle, but somehow Mom managed them both and her own household duties as well.

Even today, thirty years later, my mother still cares for eight to ten children a week. Why? So she can do little extra things for her grown children and her nine grandchildren. Things she couldn't do if she and Dad were limited to their retirement income.

An added benefit of Mom's devotion is the love and guidance she has given to scores of children for more than a quarter century. Many of them are now grown and married with children of their own, but they never fail to remember her at Christmas. Many had come from broken homes or, at best, from workaholic families in which both parents were too busy to show them the love they needed. Consequently, Mother, with her abundance of overflowing love, became the center of warmth in their lives. This too is "blue-collar Christianity."

Due to the example left me by my parents, I entered the ministry with an understanding of and a commitment to practical Christianity. It was a good thing, too, for my first church was a small congregation in the southeastern Colorado town of Holly which had a population numbering less than one thousand.

For the most part, my congregation consisted of down-to-earth people — farmers and ranchers who had weathered drought and dust, tornadoes and hail, blizzards and tough times — and they weren't overly impressed by big words and theological concepts. Their Christianity was of a more practical kind, and almost immediately I realized that my effectiveness lay not so much in the sermons I preached, but in the way I lived and how I loved. If I hadn't been a "blue-collar Christian," my congregation would not have listened to a thing I had to say.

It was my job to clean the church, take care of the yard, shovel the walks in winter and, in general, maintain the place. Oh yes, I was also expected to preach three times a week, teach a Sunday school class, lead the singing, visit the sick, and bury the dead.

Soon I found myself driving a grain truck at harvesttime and helping to round up the cattle in the fall. In between, I spent several afternoons with a wonderful old woman named Pearl who was dying of stomach cancer. I would sit with her at the kitchen table in the ranch house, drinking coffee while she told me how she and her husband had homesteaded the place. From her I learned the ministry of presence, the power of just being there, and the holy art of living until we die.

I remember another elderly lady, a longtime member of the church, whose health no longer permitted her to attend services. She lived across the alley, just south of the church, and each week I would go to her home and share the midweek Bible study with her. It was the least I could do, but she always made me feel as if I were doing her a special favor. Today I suppose we would send her a cassette tape of the service, but somehow I don't think it would be the same. Not for me anyway, for without those weekly visits my theology of the Church would be sadly lacking. The Church isn't just a weekly worship service, but a holy fellowship where the people really care about each other. She taught me that.

Fred Craddock, Professor of New Testament and Preaching at the Chandler School of Theology at Emory University, shares a personal experience which I believe explains this fellowship, this "blue-collar Christianity" as well as anything I've ever heard:

"Before I married and was serving a little mission in the Appalachians, I moved my service down to a place on Watts Bar Lake, between Chattanooga and Knoxville — a little village. It was the custom in that church at Easter to have a baptismal service. My church immerses, and this baptismal service was held in Watts Bar Lake on Easter evening at sundown. Out on a sandbar, I, with the candidates for baptism, moved into the water, and then they moved across to the shore, where the little congregation was gathered singing around the fire and cooking supper. They had constructed little booths for changing clothes, with blankets hanging, and as the candidates moved from the water, they went in and changed clothes and went to the fire in the center. And finally, last of all, I went over and changed clothes and went to the fire.

"Once we were all around the fire, this is the ritual of that tradition: Glen Hickey, always Glen, introduced the new people, gave their names, where they lived, and their work. Then the rest of us formed a circle around them while they stayed warm at the fire. The ritual was, each person in the circle gave her or his name and said this: 'My name is _____, and if you ever need somebody to do washing and ironing...' 'My name is _____, if you ever need anybody to chop wood.' 'My name is _____, if you ever need anybody to babysit.' 'My name is _____, if you ever need anybody to repair your house for you.' 'My name is _____, if you ever need anybody to sit with the sick.' 'My name is

_____, if you ever need a car to go to town.' And around the circle. Then we ate, and then we had a square dance. And at a time they knew — I didn't know — Percy Miller, with thumbs in his bibbed overalls, would stand up and say, 'It's time to go.' Everybody left, and he lingered behind and with his big shoe kicked sand over the dying fire.

"At my first experience of that, he saw me standing there still. He looked at me and said, 'Craddock, folks don't ever get any closer than this.' In that little community, they have a name for that. I've heard it in other communities, too. In that community, their name for that is church. They call that church."[2]

And so they do, for at its heart Christianity is not sermon or song but kindness — a cup of cold water in His name, if you please. Sometimes, in the moment of tragedy, it means giving comfort, sometimes encouragement to a family in crisis. At other times, we help celebrate a fortieth birthday or a twenty-fifth wedding anniversary. Just doing what we can to let our lights shine. Some places, that's called church. I call it "blue-collar Christianity."

Footnotes

1. Joyce Coloney, "Confessions of a Happy Housewife," *Reader's Digest*, Apr. 1982, p. 96.

2. Fred Craddock, "When the Roll Is Called Down Here," Preaching Today, Tape No. 50, 1987.

Chapter 1

BLUE-COLLAR CHRISTIANITY

Jesus was a blue-collar man.
He was born in a dung-infested sheep shed
to peasant parents,
and He grew up in His father's carpenter shop.

As a consequence,
He talked the language of common men,
understood the life they lived,
their little hardships,
the things they had to contend with day after day.

He knew what it was like
to struggle to make ends meet.
He was old beyond His years,
of necessity,
for as the firstborn,
He became the head of the family
at an early age
following His father's untimely death.

Life wasn't easy,
the days were long,
the work hard,
and He learned to get by on meager fare.

On top of everything else, there was the prejudice —
        whispers about the legitimacy of His birth,
                He was a Jew in a Roman world,
                        and a carpenter before it was recognized
                        as a viable trade.

Granted there was royalty in His family tree,
        'way back — and long since forgotten,
                of no interest now,
                        except to the genealogists.

He was a blue-collar man,
    not a blue-blood.

His hands were rough and calloused,
    familiar with hard work.

He was a common man among common men,
    He lived where they lived...
        fishermen,
        tax collectors,
        shepherds,
        street vendors...
    and He loved them all,
        everyone,
    outcasts of all kinds...the untouchables...
        lepers,
        lunatics,
        Samaritans,
        street people,
        and women taken in adultery.

He was concerned about the kinds of things
    that concern common people —
        children,
        paying taxes,
    bread and fish when you're hungry,
    running out of wine at your daughter's wedding.

Other things too that concern us all —
    like learning how to pray,
    not just the words,
    but really communicating with God.

And He talked a lot about loving each other,
    turning the other cheek,
        going the second mile.

He loved kids and crowds,
    celebrations and solitude,
        miracles and quiet meals with old friends.

He was a blue-collar man,
with hands hard and calloused,
from years of manual labor.

Yet His touch was gentle and healing,
    strong and reassuring.

He was a blue-collar man,
    and He calls us to be blue-collar people too.

Not psuedo-intellectuals theorizing about human need,
not bleeding hearts trapped in sentimentality,
but real, honest-to-goodness people,
    resolving human conflict,
    restoring shattered self-esteem,
    loving the loveless,
    and washing tired feet —
    even when there's no one to watch.

Jesus was a blue-collar man.

Chapter 1

BLUE-COLLAR CHRISTIANITY

Once St. Augustine was asked, "What does love look like?" He answered:

"It has hands to help others.
It has feet to hasten to the poor and needy.
It has eyes to see misery and want.
It has ears to hear the sighs and sorrow of men.
That is what love looks like."[1]

John the Beloved put it like this:

". . .Jesus Christ laid down his life for us. And we ought to lay down our lives for our brothers. If anyone has material possessions and sees his brother in need but has no pity on him, how can the love of God be in him? Dear children, let us not love with words or tongue but with actions and in truth."

1 John 3:16-18

Now that's what I call "blue-collar Christianity." No fancy words, no doctrine or dogma, not even stained glass or steeples. Just love with its sleeves rolled up, caring enough to get involved, taking a chance on getting hurt or being let down, yet knowing that taking the risk is better than playing it safe and maybe never knowing either the pain or the joy of really loving.

According to Frederick Buechner, prominent Presbyterian minister and author, "Compassion is the sometimes fatal capacity for feeling what it is like to live inside somebody's else's skin. It is the knowledge that there can never really be any peace and joy for me until there is peace and joy finally for you too."[2]

Realizing that sobering reality, my staff and I began a ninety-minute, live, call-in radio broadcast called "Straight From the Heart." It was people-centered rather than issue-centered. We focused on things like grief and loss, growing old, divorce, the need to belong, and similar topics. Soon we were inundated with calls from hurting people. It was readily apparent that we couldn't handle all of their needs by phone, so we established a counseling center and organized support groups of various kinds.

Our center was staffed by "blue-collar Christians," people who for the most part had discovered, like Buechner, that they couldn't really enjoy life unless others enjoyed it too. Of course, this commitment generated enormous pressure for the counselors because, with an attitude like that, it's virtually impossible to ignore a single cry for help.

One of our counselors wrote me a letter in which he shared a typical experience:

"I was interrupted last night. I had just returned from a long trip. . .tired, wanting to rest, and the phone rang. It was Hector. Would I meet him for coffee? I knew I should go, so I went; and now I'm glad I did. There in a secluded booth sat a lonely man, wrecked with guilt and fear, feeling little worth, bruised and hurt by his past. And there I was, attempting to give out just a little of all that had been ministered to me. Slowly, this man began to see hope, to get a little clearer view of God's true character, to feel he belongs to this thing we call humanity.

"For a moment I realized a little more of God's Kingdom. For a moment I understood a little more of Christ's ministry. For a moment I felt the Church as it's supposed to be — for a moment I was the Church!"

And that's what love looks like. It's "blue-collar Christianity," the Gospel in shoe leather, compassion with its sleeves rolled up, caring enough to get involved! It has hands to help others.

Unfortunately, it's a lot easier, and more acceptable, to limit our Christian service to "spiritual" things. You know — Bible studies, choir, fellowship groups with "our kind of people." Nice things, safe things, which let us feel like we are serving but without running the risk of getting our hands dirty.

It's a subtle trap, and one not easily discerned. A trap in which we tend to mistake busyness for commitment, and religious activity for true spiritual activism.

Ruth Harris Calkin exposes my own propensity for platform ministry when she makes this confession:

"You know, Lord, how I serve You
With great emotional fervor
In the limelight.
You know how eagerly I speak for You
At a women's club.
You know how I effervesce when I promote
A fellowship group.
You know my genuine enthusiasm
At a bible study.

"But how would I react, I wonder
If You pointed to a basin of water
And asked me to wash the calloused feet
Of a bent and wrinkled old woman,
Day after day,
Month after month,
In a room where nobody saw
And nobody knew."[3]

Now that's what I'm talking about — our tendency to seek highly visible forms of ministry rather than seeking ways to help the hurting.

It's really not a new problem. In fact, the disciples struggled with it themselves. They were eager to share the limelight with Jesus, jockeying for the best position, clamoring to sit at His right hand or at His left, but unwilling to wash each other's feet.

I do think, however, that this tendency is more pronounced in our day due, at least in part, to the proliferation of media ministries with their high visibility and slick formats. They have given us a new model for ministry, one in which performance has replaced service, in which talent is more important than compassion.

Let me hasten to add that I do not intend to categorically indict all media ministries. In fact, several of them are deeply committed to serving and have developed a grassroots network of compassionate people who are providing one-on-one ministry, including food and clothing distribution, as well as prayer and counseling. The problem is not necessarily with the ministries as much as it is with our perception of them, and our inherent need to be recognized. Often our desire for public ministry is more a reflection of our need to be seen than a genuine concern for the needs of others.

Does that sound harsh? I hope not, for that is not my intent. I do feel, though, that my conclusions are accurate.

Let me give you an example. About three years ago, I became acquainted with one of our "Straight From the Heart" listeners. She called in seeking emotional support, not just once but several times. Her husband had suffered a stroke which had left him paralyzed; consequently, he required custodial care twenty-four hours a day. The couple had no family within driving distance nor could they afford to place the husband in a nursing home. As a result, the wife was the only caregiver and a virtual prisoner in her own home.

In addition to the emotional support she sought, she really needed someone to relieve her for a few hours each week so she could get out of the house. Unfortunately, when I suggested this to a number of those people who were supposedly looking for a church in which they could get involved, they turned pale and mumbled something about that not really being the kind of ministry they had in mind.

That's tragic, for when we neglect humanity's suffering, we neglect Jesus Himself:

" 'Then he will say to those on his left, "Depart from me, you who are cursed...For I was hungry and you gave me nothing to eat, I was thirsty and you gave me nothing to drink, I was a stranger and you did not invite me in, I needed clothes and you did not clothe me, I was sick and in prison and you did not look after me."

" 'They also will answer, "Lord, when did we see you hungry or thirsty or a stranger or needing clothes or sick or in prison, and did not help you?"

" 'He will reply, "I tell you the truth, whatever you did not do for one of the least of these, you did not do for me." ' "

Matthew 25:41-45

And if it's true that by neglecting the "least of these" we have neglected Jesus Himself (and it is, for in some mysterious way the poor and needy are indeed God in disguise), then it must be equally true that when we reach out to the "least of these" we are also reaching out to Him. Or as Jesus said, " '...I tell you the truth, whatever you did for one of the least of these brothers of mine, you did for me' " (Matt. 25:40).

This theme is oft repeated in the devotional classics. For instance, there's Flaubert's story of St. Julian, L'Hospitalier:

"As a child Julian loved to wander in the forests and loved all animals and living things. He lived on a great estate, and his

29

parents worshipped him; they wanted him to have everything in the world. His father bought him the finest horses, bows and arrows, and taught him to hunt. To kill the very animals he had loved so much. And that was too bad, because Julian discovered that he liked to kill. He was only happy after a day of the bloodiest slaughter. The murdering of beasts and birds became a mania, and after first admiring his skill, his neighbors loathed and feared him for his bloodlust.

"Somehow or other Julian killed his mother and father. A hunting accident? Something like that, something terrible. He became a pariah and a penitent. He wandered the world barefoot and in rags, seeking forgiveness. He grew old and ill. One cold night he was waiting by a river for a boatman to row him across...Because Julian was dying. While he waited, a hideous old man appeared. He was a leper, and his eyes were running sores, his mouth rotting and foul. Julian didn't know it, but this repulsive evil-looking old man was God. And God tested him to see if all his sufferings had truly changed Julian's savage heart. He told Julian He was cold, and asked to share his blanket, and Julian did; then the leper wanted Julian to embrace Him, and Julian did; then He made a final request — He asked Julian to kiss his diseased and rotting lips. Julian did. Whereupon Julian and the old leper, who was suddenly transformed into a radiant shining vision, ascended together to heaven. And so it was that Julian became St. Julian."[4]

And that's one of the ways God's grace works in each of our lives as well, one of the ways He frees us from our selfish selves. He gives us opportunities to serve, chances to share our blanket and our blessings with those less fortunate than we. And like Julian, we too become saints, that is, we are given a heart of compassion, hands to help others, and feet to hasten to the poor and needy.

One of the things I admire most about the congregation I now serve is their compassion, their willingness to give of themselves and their resources, their willingness to get involved. It's not something we've really organized, not another program, as much as it is individuals responding on their own, out of a heart of love and compassion.

For instance, at Christmastime I received a call from a man in the church who wanted to know if I knew of a needy family, someone with whom he and his family could share Christmas.

"What," I asked him, "do you have in mind?"

"Well," he said, "I thought you might be aware of a special situation, one of the 'Straight From the Heart' listeners perhaps, a family who won't have much of a Christmas unless they get some help. What we would like to do is buy some groceries, and some presents for the children. And if it's all right, we would like to take it to them. Not so we can appear to be great philanthropists, but in order to make it somehow personal. We don't just want to give groceries and things. We want to give something of ourselves as well."

I knew just the family, a desperate situation. A few weeks earlier, the mother had called during one of our broadcasts and had shared her painful story.

She was divorced, trying to rear two children alone and unemployed. To make matters worse, her youngest son had leukemia. In addition to the obvious financial difficulties and the trauma of her son's illness, she was pregnant. The father was a married man, a leader in the church. She never had any intention of becoming involved with him. It had just sort of happened. While he was providing pastoral care for her, during a critical time in her son's illness, an emotional bond had been formed between them. In a moment of weakness, this bond resulted in a sexual encounter which was completely unpremeditated.

Recognizing that their actions were sinful and potentially destructive, they immediately terminated their relationship, but the damage had already been done. As soon as she realized that she was pregnant, she decided to leave the church rather than risk damaging the father's family or jeopardizing his position in the church. Now she was alone, without family or friends or a support system of any kind.

I contacted the woman by telephone and after getting her permission I made the necessary arrangements. That was the last I heard about the situation until a few days after Christmas when that generous couple dropped by the office to give me a report. They said it had been one of the most meaningful experiences of their lives, and I can believe it. There's something about an unselfish act that is its own reward. You can't give love away without getting it back, in good measure, pressed down, and running over.

They (that couple and their three children) had gone out there to make Christmas for that desperate mother and her two small sons and discovered instead that God had made Christmas for them. Years from now, when their own children have long since forgotten other Christmases, they will recall the magic of that experience, the magic of making Christmas for someone less fortunate than themselves.

Only God knows what their act of kindness meant to that destitute mother and her two small sons. I have to believe though that their presence meant more than the presents they brought. Because as bad as that little family needed groceries, as poverty-stricken as they were, as bleak as their Christmas might have been, what they needed more than anything else was the warmth, the reality of genuine fellowship.

Bob Benson, in his little book *Come Share the Being*, relates a tragic story which graphically illustrates just how much we really need each other. He writes:

"We bought an old building and remodeled it for offices and warehouse space. The electrician who did the work was named Richard. He was such a talker that after a while somebody in the building started calling him 'Motormouth.' He always had a smile and a ready answer to any question, serious or joking. He was a joy to have in the building. In a year or so we were making some additional changes that would require wiring and I asked if anyone had called Richard.

"Somebody said, 'Didn't you hear about Richard?' 'No, I didn't.' 'Well, about two months ago his partner went by the trailer park to go to work with him and Richard said, "I'll just meet you up at the job in about twenty minutes."

" 'And Richard went back to the trailer. He had been arguing with his wife and went back to the bedroom and came back and touched her on the shoulder as she stood at the sink. She turned just in time to see him pull the trigger of the pistol he had pressed against his head.'

"Richard, 'Motormouth,' always joking, always laughing, always talking, always willing to be the butt of our jokes, was dead. I'd asked him lots of times how he was doing, but I guess I had never asked him in such a way that made him want to tell me.

"Life in a way is like those electric bump cars at the amusement park. We just run at each other and smile and bump and away we go.

"How are you doing —
      bump, bump,

Hi, Motormouth —
      bump, bump,

Great, fantastic —
      bump, bump, bump,

And somebody slips out and dies because there is no one to talk to.
      bump, bump, bump."[5]

What a haunting picture of our broken world. Hundreds of hurting people pretending to "have it all together." Laughing, talking, hiding their pain behind a superficial gaiety. I can't help but wonder how many people I've bumped into, how many times I've asked how they were doing, but not in a way that made them want to tell me. How many of them slipped out into the night and died, just a little on the inside, because they had no one to talk to. I mean really talk to.

Yet, even as they pretend, with such clever and convincing aplomb, they are desperately hoping that we won't be taken in by their empty act, that we won't let them get away with it.

Rabbi Dov Peretz Elkins writes:

"Don't be fooled by me. Don't be fooled by the face I wear. I wear a mask. I wear a thousand masks — masks that I am afraid to take off; and none of them are me.

"Pretending is an art that is second nature to me, but don't be fooled. For my sake, don't be fooled. I give the impression that I am secure, that all is sunny and unruffled within me as well as without; that confidence is my name and coolness is my game, that the water is calm and I am in command; and that I need no one. But don't believe me, please. My surface may seem smooth, but my surface is my mask, my ever-varying and ever-concealing mask.

"Beneath lies no smugness, no complacence. Beneath dwells, the real me in confusion, in fear, in aloneness. But I hide that. I don't want anybody to know it. I panic at the thought of my weakness and fear being exposed. That's why I frantically create a mask to hide behind — a nonchalant, sophisticated facade — to help me pretend, to shield me from the glance that knows. But such a glance is precisely my salvation, my only salvation, and I know it. That is, if it's followed by acceptance; if it's followed by love.

"It's the only thing that can liberate me from myself, from my own self-built prison wall, from the barriers I so painstakingly erect. It's the only thing that will assure me of what I can't assure myself — that I am really something...

"Who am I, you may wonder. I am someone you know very well. I am every man you meet. I am every woman you meet. I am every child you meet. I am right in front of you. Please...love me."[6]

"Blue-collar Christians" have ears to hear those desperate but unspoken cries and the capacity to respond in love. They have eyes to see, not only humanity's obvious brokenness, not only its physical sufferings and need, but its hidden hurts as well. The little rejections that have become deep self-doubt, the insecurities, the loss of self-esteem.

Such caring people have developed the "glance that knows" and the love that makes it liberating instead of devastating.

And real Christians don't just bump into people. They take time to get to know each other realizing that you can't truly love someone unless you know them.

Madeleine L'Engle writes in *Walking on Water*:

"My son-in-law, Alan Jones, told me a story of a Hasidic rabbi, renowned for his piety. He was unexpectedly confronted one day by one of his devoted youthful disciples. In a burst of feeling, the young disciple exclaimed, 'My master, I love you!' The ancient teacher looked up from his books and asked his fervent disciple, 'Do you know what hurts me, my son?'

"The young man was puzzled. Composing himself, he stuttered, 'I don't understand your question, Rabbi. I am trying to tell you how much you mean to me, and you confuse me with irrelevant questions.'

" 'My question is neither confusing nor irrelevant,' rejoined the rabbi, 'for if you do not know what hurts me, how can you truly love me?' "[7]

"Blue-collar Christians" know what hurts people, probably because they have been hurt themselves. But rather than becoming bitter, thay have made peace with their pain, made it an ally instead of an enemy. And now they have "hands to help others" and "feet to hasten to the poor and needy." They have "eyes to see misery and want," and "ears to hear the sighs and sorrows of men."

How "blue-collar" are you?

If it seems you have fallen short of that high ideal, don't be too hard on yourself, don't give up. Almost no one loves like that naturally, at least not at first. In the beginning even our "Christian" love is selfish. It seems we are always loving in ways which feel good to us, ways which make us feel loving rather than in ways which make others feel loved. And remember, we learn to be "holy lovers" by loving, by doing it, not just by reading about it.

How, you may be asking, can I get started? Begin with prayer. Honestly confess your misunderstandings and shortcomings:

"My world's too little, Lord.
I've no room for other cultures.
No time for Cambodian refugees,
or starving Ethiopians,
or even the broken family down the street.

"My world's too little, Lord.
I was reared in a Christian home,
    and I'm a charter member of my church.
I've no room for the orphans of this world.
No time for the homeless,
or the unemployed,
or even the faceless street people
who huddle in corners to escape the cold.

"Yet, try as I will,
I can't escape the empty look in their eyes.
T.V. specials,
    magazine articles,
    missions conventions,
        all bring them back to me.

"My world's not too little, Lord,
    just too crowded.

Empty my heart of vain ambition.
Free my mind of carnal dreams.
Fill me with compassion and concern
for those who know You not.
Whether they be
      Cambodian refugees,
           faceless street people,
                or the divorcee from down the street."

Now look around you, I mean really look. What do you see? Probably needy people within arm's reach, right there in your own family. A spouse you've been too busy to love, a teenager you've never taken time to understand, a child who hardly knows you. Or maybe it's the person you work with. The one you've written off as antisocial, the troublemaker. Do you have any idea why he's so angry, so defensive? What about the misfit you worship with, the person who is always on the outside looking in, the gal nobody likes? You know, the one who talks too loud, the one who tries too hard. You can get started by loving that person.

" 'Somewhere in the world,' Dr. Elton Trueblood has written, 'there should be a society consciously and deliberately devoted to the task of seeing how love can be made real, and demonstrating love in practice.' "[8]

It won't necessarily be easy. Often the people who need our love the most are the very people who are the most unlovable. Like the wealthy, self-sufficient divorcee in Katherine Anne Porter's *Ship of Fools,* they too are crying for love even when their behavior is hostile or defensive. "Love me," they cry. "Love me in spite of all! Whether or not I love you, whether I am fit to love, whether you are able to love, even if there is no such thing as love, love me!"[9]

Sometimes it may seem we love in vain, but take heart, all is not lost. Even if others never respond to our love, we are better for having loved them. The very act of loving has enriched us, made us more Christlike. And, not infrequently, love works its miracle and another cynical person is made new, another bitter heart is healed.

"The late Dr. Karl Menninger of the Menninger Clinic in Topeka, Kansas, decided that most of his patients were there because they had not loved or been loved, or both. As a result, he called in his staff and told them that above all else they were to love. Every contact with patients was to be a love contact. From the top psychiatrists down to the electricians and window-cleaners, all must manifest love. They did so. Six months later he discovered that the expected hospitalization time of his patients had been cut by 50 percent.

"One woman sat day after day in her rocking chair without saying a word to anybody. The doctor called a nurse and told her, 'All I'm asking you to do is to love her until she gets well.' The nurse accepted the challenge. She got another rocking chair, sat alongside the woman, and rocked without saying anything. The third day the patient spoke, and in a week she was out of her shell and on her way to health."[10]

Now that's "blue-collar Christianity" at its very best. Sharing another's silence and sorrow, bearing their burden with them, loving them in their lovelessness. And love does it again! Works another miracle, restores another despairing soul to the reality of life.

Footnotes

1. St. Augustine, quoted in *Dawnings, Finding God's Light in the Darkness,* edited by Phyllis Hobe (New York: Guideposts Associates, Inc., 1981), p. 96.

2. Frederick Buechner, quoted in *Disciplines for the Inner Life* by Bob Benson and Michael Benson (Waco: Word Books Publisher, 1985), p. 312.

3. Ruth Harris Calkin, *Tell Me Again Lord, I Forget* (Elgin: David C. Cook Publishing Co., 1974), p. 14.

4. Truman Capote, *Music for Chameleons* (New York: Random House, 1980), pp. 260, 261.

5. Benson and Benson, pp. 311, 312.

6. Dov Peretz Elkins, *Glad to Be Me,* (Englewood Cliffs: Prentice-Hall, Inc., 1976), pp. 28, 29.

7. Madeleine L'Engle, *Walking On Water* (Wheaton: Harold Shaw Publishers, 1980), pp. 70,71.

8. Gordon C. Hunter, *When the Walls Come Tumblin' Down* (Waco: Word Books Publisher, 1970). p. 26.

9. Katherine Anne Porter, *Ship of Fools* (Boston: Little, Brown & Co., 1962).

10. Hunter, p. 22.

Chapter 2

THE COMPASSIONATE TOUCH

I'm deeply disturbed, Lord,
by man's inhumanity to man.
The slum lord's exploitation of the poor,
    immigration policies which imprison,
        racism which punishes a person
            for the color of his skin.

I'm deeply disturbed, Lord,
by man's inhumanity to man.
Wife abuse,
    incest,
        and child pornography.

I'm deeply disturbed, Lord,
by man's inhumanity to man.
His carnal cruelty,
    careless words that cut to the core,
        the look that kills,
            public humiliation.

I'm deeply disturbed, Lord,
by man's inhumanity to man.
His insensitivity and self-centeredness,
    the need to win,
        to always be right,
            to come out on top.

I'm deeply disturbed, Lord,
by man's inhumanity to man.
There's got to be a better way,
this dog-eat-dog world just won't make it.
A man can't go it alone,
    he can't go through life trusting no one.
He has to have somebody to talk to,
    someone he can confide in,

at least one person with whom he can share
his heart.

He has to have somebody who believes in him,
someone who sees the greatness within,
at least one person who knows his dreams
and dreams them with him.

Let me be that one, Lord,
the person to confide in,
the one who sees the possibilities,
the one who speaks to the greatness within.
I can't do much about economic exploitation
or repressive political policies,
but I can listen with love,
lend a helping hand,
share a meal,
and speak an affirming word
in the moment of despair.
That may not seem like much,
I mean, it's not a cure-all for
man's inhumanity to man,
but if I can make just one person's load lighter,
one person's dream a little brighter,
if I can dare to give into goodness now and then,
then maybe, just maybe,
someone else will be inspired to try goodness too,
and who knows what might happen then!

THE COMPASSIONATE TOUCH

A wise man once said, "When I was a young man, I admired clever men. Now that I am old, I admire kind men."

Though I'm neither old nor particularly wise, I think I know what he meant. When I was younger, I too admired clever men, and aspired to be like them. Now that I'm older, and have had a chance to live a little, cleverness doesn't seem nearly so appealing. Clever people are generally self-centered and self-serving. They are quick to find the easy answer, the path of least resistance. They amuse the crowd with their quick wit and ready reply, but they seem somehow to lack compassion. Kindness, on the other hand, wears well. Genuinely good men may not be as flashy nor as entertaining as their clever counterparts, but over the long haul they always prove their worth.

The Bible gives us several examples of good men and women, godly persons whose lives radiated with His love and compassion. As such, they have become examples for us, models.

Fred Smith, in his book, *You and Your Network*,[1] draws a distinction between a hero and a model. A hero, he concludes, is a person who shows you who he can be. A model, on the other hand, is a person who shows you what you can be.

Barnabas, of New Testament fame, was such a man. Acts 11:24 says, "He was a good man, full of the Holy Spirit and faith. . . ." He is, perhaps, the most outstanding example of genuine goodness in all of the New Testament, an example of the extra-ordinary things God can do with the most ordinary person.

According to early church history, he was a Levite from Cyprus whose real name was Joseph. The apostles changed his name to Barnabas, which means "Son of Encouragement," probably because he was a constant source of strength and affirmation. That happened shortly after the founding of the church in Jerusalem, and thereafter no one called him anything else because everywhere he went he brought encouragement and hope.

He makes me think of Winston Churchill, in the midst of the Battle of Britain in the Second World War, when everyone was at the point of despair. Morning after morning, following yet another Nazi air attack, Mr. Churchill would don his black coat and black bowler, and stride resolutely over the rubble reminding his people, "We have just begun to fight." Night after night, the radio waves would carry his message of hope to the battered British population.

"When I look back at the perils which have been already overcome, upon the great mountain waves through which the ship has driven, when I remember all that has gone right," he told them, "I am encouraged to feel we need not be afraid that the tempest will overcome. Let it roar, let it rage, we shall come through."[2]

Writing in *Saturday Review*, Norman Cousins said that Churchill's greatness was his ability to "speak to the strength inside of people and to cause that strength then to come into being." He said that because of Winston Churchill, millions of people discovered what it means to come fully alive: "They knew that they faced total danger, but he helped them find their capacity for total response. They also learned that it was far less painful to sit the whole of themselves against the monstrous force than it was to sit on the sidelines half alive."[3]

That is what Barnabas did for the early church. He encouraged them when the fury of the Sanhedrin was loosed. See him as he goes from house to house, meeting with small groups of believers, leading them in prayer, assuring them that God has everything under control, that no matter what happens God will use it, turn it for their good and the good of the Kingdom!

At first the persecution was directed mainly toward the apostles. Almost daily they were threatened, flogged, and sometimes even imprisoned. That was bad enough, but it soon spread and "...a great persecution broke out against the church at Jerusalem, and all except the apostles were scattered throughout Judea and Samaria...Saul began to destroy the church. Going from house to house, he dragged off men and women and put them in prison" (Acts 8:1,3).

As a consequence, Barnabas became an itinerant. Anywhere there were believers, there he was, the son of encouragement, comforting and encouraging, rallying their faith. And only God knows what losses his tireless encouragement spared the infant church, how many men and women remained faithful because of the strength of his presence.

His most notable beneficiary was none other than the infamous Saul of Tarsus, the very one whose violent persecution scattered the infant church. On his way to Damascus, to do damage to the Body of Christ, Saul was miraculously converted. Upon his return to Jerusalem, he attempted to "...join the disciples, but they were all afraid of him, not believing that he really was a disciple. But Barnabas took him and brought him to the apostles. He told them how Saul on his journey had seen the Lord and that the Lord had spoken to him, and how in Damascus he had preached fearlessly in the name of Jesus. So Saul stayed with them and moved about freely in Jerusalem, speaking boldly in the name of the Lord" (Acts 9:26-28).

Saul, of course, came to be known as Paul the Apostle. During his lifetime he planted churches throughout the known world. He was a tireless missionary who was undeterred by either hardship or persecution. Nothing, absolutely nothing, kept him from preaching the gospel of Jesus Christ. When the authorities imprisoned him, he converted the jailer and penned much of the New Testament. From his cell in Rome he wrote, "Now I want you to know, brothers, that what has happened to me has really served to advance the gospel" (Phil. 1:12). Yet were it not for Barnabas, we might never have heard of Paul the Apostle, there might not have been an Apostle Paul.

It's not hard to imagine what might have happened if Barnabas had not taken a chance and spoken on Saul's behalf. Very few of us can grow and mature as believers without the fellowship of the Body of Christ. Saul was no exception. He too needed the security and encouragement afforded by the disciples. Without their fellowship, he might well have lost his newfound faith, or, at best, have faded into obscurity.

It was also Barnabas who gave Saul his start in the ministry. Acts 11:25,26 says: "Then Barnabas went to Tarsus to look for Saul, and when he found him, he brought him to Antioch. So for a whole year Barnabas and Saul met with the church and taught great numbers of people...."

Sometimes the most significant thing we can do for the Kingdom of God is to encourage others. Only God knows how far-reaching our investment in their lives may be. When Barnabas took time to encourage Saul, I doubt that he ever imagined that his kindness would affect believers for twenty centuries to come, but it did and it does. Never make the mistake of belittling the eternal value of the ministry which you invest in another.

"In the little village of Blantyre, Scotland, a common laborer by the name of David Hogg taught a small Sunday school class of young boys year after year with a devotion that was the wonder of all who knew him. Out from that class went a young man, David

Livingstone, to the vast continent of Africa to wear out his life, going through the jungles from village to village, witnessing to the Christian faith. Some time later another missionary came to one of these same villages where Livingstone had been years before, and he told of the life and ministry of Jesus Christ. An old lady, however, interrupted him, and said, 'That man has been here!'

"Think if it, men and women: a village church in far away Scotland; a little boy in the sanctuary; a consecrated Sunday school teacher; and you get the footprints of Christ in and out of the muddy villages of Africa."[4] And that's the far-reaching power of encouragement!

Most of us will never have either the opportunity, or the awesome responsibility, afforded Winston Churchill of inspiring and maintaining the morale of an entire nation in its hour of greatest crisis. Nor will many of us be used of God, as Barnabas was, to sustain a church besieged by persecution. But life does afford each of us the opportunity to be a source of encouragement to others in their moment of crisis. Frequently it will be members of our own family, our spouse or our children. The way we respond can make the difference between a productive and useful life or one lived without hope.

John L. Gwaltney is a professor of anthropology at Syracuse University. Besides honorary doctorates from Bucknell University and Upsala College, he holds a Ph.D. degree from Columbia University. He is also the author of *The Thrice Shy: Cultural Accommodation to Blindness and Drylongso: A Self-Portrait of Black America*. Those are significant credentials for anyone, but for one who was born on the eve of the Great Depression, blind, and black, they are absolutely incredible.

How did he do it?

His mother was a "Barnabas," an encourager, and she gave him the gift of self-confidence. She taught him the difference between what he thought he could do and what she knew he could do. He says, "I have my mother to thank for my never having felt like a poor blind boy. . . .When I was a young child she told me, 'I'm sorry to my heart that your eyes are not good. If I could, I would give you mine. But you have a good mind and you will learn to think or my name is not Mabel Harper Gwaltney.' "[5]

She was tireless in her efforts to see that he never succumbed to either self-pity or the dark and limiting confines that blindness imposed on so many. At the first hint of a whine in his voice, she could and did become a firm disciplinarian. Once, when he was just barely five years old, nothing seemed to please him.

"The more attention I received the more I wanted," he writes. "When I asked my mother to read for the third time a story I knew by heart, she told me to come over and sit by her.

" 'Nothing can content you today,' she said. 'Now, everybody feels that way sometimes and maybe you will feel that way more often than most people. I think you are feeling sad and don't know what to do with yourself because you can't see, but you must learn to content yourself.' She gave me some stiff covers from her old magazines, some pins and a pillow, and I contented myself by pricking Braille pictures in the thick paper. When I had explained my pictures to her, she said, 'Good, now don't be asking me for time just to see if you can get it.' "[6]

Of another time, he writes, "When I disobeyed a plainly heard and understood important order, corporal punishment was as predictable as the rising of the sun. One time the inevitable consequence of my rampant disobedience brought tears to the eyes of my mother's friend, Miss Nelly, whose chief delight was in spoiling me. Miss Nelly's silent tears of misplaced pity said plainer than words, 'Mabel, how could you do that to a poor blind boy?' My mother said, 'Nelly, there is not a thing wrong with this child's ears.' "[7]

Though she was infinitely more at home in her own oral tradition, she addressed a dignified written request for assistance to the nation's First Lady, Mrs. Eleanor Roosevelt, and received a swift reply which resulted in a local chain of educational services for the blind being made available for her son. In addition to her determined efforts to make sure that blindness did not limit him, to make sure he received every opportunity that training and education could afford, she also sought and tried every treatment there was which promised even the slightest chance of a cure.

As is often the case, her determined efforts shaped his character and sharpened his mind without making an impression on his consciousness. It was many years before he was even dimly aware of the extent and generosity of her investment of time and energy.

"As the velvet hood of the honorary Doctorate of Letters from my alma mater settled upon my shoulders," he recalls, "I remembered my profound indebtedness to my mother, who had died 28 years before, just as I was about to graduate from college. It was her diligence, imagination and insistence upon excellence which made me think that the life of a scholar was attainable in spite of my blindness."[8]

"Miz Mabel" (as she was affectionately known) was a "Barnabas" in her own right — a mother of encouragement.

In addition to being a constant source of encouragement, Barnabas was also a generous man. For him the world's needs were his own, and his resources the world's resources. Acts 4:36,37 and 35 says, "Joseph, a Levite from Cyprus, whom the apostles called Barnabas. . .sold a field he owned and brought the money and put it at the apostles' feet. . . .and it was distributed to anyone as he had need."

Recently, I heard missionary Larry Smith describe the desperate plight of Bangladesh, the world's poorest and most densely populated country. As he preached, it seemed the Lord spoke to my heart and I realized, maybe for the first time, the real cause of world poverty and hunger. The problem is not a shortage of resources; there is plenty of land, raw materials, wealth and food for all. The problem is a *disproportionate distribution* of available resources; a small percentage of the world's population controls — and consumes — far too much of its material and spiritual goods.

About three years ago, we were involved in a capital funds campaign in preparation for building our new facilities. We called the campaign Operation Faith because we weren't just focusing on money. Rather, we were explaining the vision of the church and challenging our congregation to believe with us. Of course, those who caught the vision were encouraged to give that it might become a reality. For most of us that meant giving money, time and talent. For Ben and Rochelle it meant something more, much more.

Ben's sister needed a kidney transplant and he was a possible donor. From a safe distance that may not seem like such a significant thing, but when you get right down to it, it's an altogether different matter. First there's the risk of major surgery, then the lifelong consequences of living with one kidney instead of two, and the increased danger due to illness or injury. What if something happened to that one remaining kidney?

Suddenly it wasn't a theoretical question any more but a matter of life and death. Ben had to consider his wife and their future children. How would this decision affect them in the long run? Then there were the "nitty-gritty" things to consider, like time off from work without pay, the trip to Minneapolis, the loss of vacation time, the pain of surgery itself.

Ultimately, Ben felt God was asking him to trust Him with his life, his kidney. After much prayer, he concluded that he had no right to live with two kidneys when his sister had none, when his sister was facing death unless she had a transplant. He could have said let someone else do it, another family member. He could have encouraged his sister to seek a cadaver kidney. But he didn't. Love wouldn't allow it — his love for her, and for God. And so Ben and Rochelle decided that he should donate his kidney, lay down his life for his sister.

It wasn't a decision they made lightly. It wasn't something they could "undo" once it was done. It was a decision that had to be made based on a "worse case scenario," on what might happen if Ben were in an accident or contacted a serious illness. Still, having considered all of that, having considered the worst possible consequences, Ben and Rochelle went ahead with the operation because that was what they thought God wanted them to do, and because it was what they wanted to do too.

Most of us won't ever have to make a decision like that. Our decisions will be less dramatic, but no less significant. We will have to decide what to keep for ourselves and what to share with the world, what's a reasonable lifestyle in light of the needy in our own churches, and in our own country, not to mention the desperate plight of the people of Bangladesh.

Sometimes we are tempted to dismiss the world's need, and our responsibility, by reasoning that whatever we gave it would be far too little even to make a dent in world poverty. Writing in *Human Options,* Norman Cousins addresses this very issue:

"Certainly it is true that behind every human being who cries out for help there may be a million or more entitled to attention. But this is the poorest of all reasons for not helping the person whose cries you hear. Where, then, does one begin or stop? How to choose? How to determine which one of a million sounds surrounding you is more deserving than the rest? Do not concern yourself in such speculations. You will never know; you will never need to know. Reach out and take hold of the one who happens to be nearest. If you are never able to help or save another, at least you will have saved one."[9]

And that, I believe, is the New Testament definition of goodness — doing what you can for those you encounter, for those who pass through your life.

Romans 12:13 says, "Share with God's people who are in need. Practice hospitality." And not just with God's people either, but with every man, with strangers, ". . .for by so doing some people have entertained angels without knowing it" (Heb. 13:2); and, "If your enemy is hungry, feed him; if he is thirsty, give him something to drink. . . . Do not be overcome by evil, but overcome evil with good" (Rom. 12:20,21).

Don't make the mistake though of confusing goodness with weakness; there's a world of difference. Barnabas was a good man, but he was not a weak man. He was a generous man, but he was not a "soft touch." In fact, when the occasion called for it, he could be downright tough. Take the dispute he had with Paul over John Mark, for instance.

"Some time later Paul said to Barnabas, 'Let us go back and visit the brothers in all the towns where we preached the word of the Lord and see how they are doing.' Barnabas wanted to take John, also called Mark, with them, but Paul did not think it wise to take him, because he had deserted them in Pamphylia and had not continued with them in the work. They had such a sharp disagreement that they parted company. Barnabas took Mark and sailed for Cyprus, but Paul chose Silas and left, commended by the brothers to the grace of the Lord" (Acts 15:36-40).

Sometimes being a good man means taking a stand for what is right, even at the risk of a friendship. Note, however, that Barnabas was not taking a stand for himself or his own personal interests. He was risking his friendship with Paul on behalf of John Mark, not unlike the way he had spent his influence with the apostles on behalf of Paul himself some years earlier. His actions really shouldn't surprise us for he couldn't have done anything else and still have been the Barnabas we have come to know and love.

Only God knows how many people have been saved for the Kingdom through the direct intervention of good men like Barnabas, men who were willing to take a chance on an apparent failure, willing to give a man another opportunity to prove himself. If a man has any strength of character, any potential for goodness, he cannot help but rise to such an occasion.

Take John Mark, for instance. Despite his earlier abandonment of the ministry, we don't remember him as a failure, but as the man who came back. As such, he has been an inspiration and an encouragement to every man who has ever sought a second chance. He became a close friend of the great Apostle Peter and the author of the Gospel which bears his name. Eventually even Paul recognized his worth and wrote in one of his last epistles, "...Get Mark and bring him with you, because he is helpful to me in my ministry" (2 Tim. 4:11).

And then there's the story of Marla, as told by best-selling author Ann Kiemel in *It's Incredible:*

"...once an unwed mother, now in her second marriage,
    a minister's wife, remade, and
        being used by God's Spirit in her little
            piece of the world.

"marla understands when people ask her about forgiveness. she first married when she was seventeen years old. it seemed so perfect, so right...but while she was pregnant with their first child, she discovered that her husband was having affairs with other women.

"one day, before the baby was born, david was on a new motorcycle when a car hit him...and his leg had to be amputated. he was bitter. when the baby came, he threatened to kill her when she cried, and to kill marla too.

"eventually, she had to take the baby and flee for safety. she began to work in a restaurant within walking distance of the apartment.

"a policeman would come in to eat on his rounds, and was friendly to her...and they found themselves strongly attracted to each other. even though he was married and had two little daughters, the attraction was too strong to resist.

"marla, brokenhearted, moved away...but wherever she moved, larry the policeman found her...

"she loved him, and before long, she was pregnant with his baby. moving again, she found a duplex that would be cheaper and offer more room, and she decided to have the baby and not intrude on larry's marriage.

"the couple that shared the other side of the duplex were out working on a fence, when marla went out to get acquainted. in the course of the conversation the neighbors mentioned they had to go get ready for their church softball game.

"marla asked which church...
> well, could she go with them on Sunday?
> this church-going couple was shocked.
here was a hungry neighbor who had to INITIATE the invitation to church.

"the people in that little church loved marla, and nurtured her. they helped her learn that Jesus would forgive her even though she couldn't forgive herself.

"she gave birth to a boy, and named him after his father...whom she loved but
> had no idea where he was. marla still
> hadn't finished high school. she went at night,
> and worked hard. even so, she ended up
> on welfare.
and then
out of nowhere
larry showed up again.
it had been fifteen months.

"this frightened, burdened young woman was lonely and vulnerable...and her one sexual
> encounter in fifteen months
> > put her back into pregnancy.

" 'oh, ann i couldn't believe it. i wanted to die.
> i was not only a disgrace to my family, but
> > to God. i claimed to be a Christian, and i

loved the Lord Jesus, but i could only seem to
   make messes.

"i wanted to run. i couldn't face my church family.
i had two children now, and we could hardly survive.'

"she went to the bathroom, and started to take every
pill she could find...
suddenly it seemed that the whole room
       was filled with the presence of God.
   she began to think of the words to a song
       that she had recently learned in church...

   " 'amazing grace...how sweet the sound...
   that saved a WRETCH like me...i once was
       lost...but now, I'm found...
   was blind, but now i see.' "

"there, in that bathroom, Jesus came
to marla. there...
   amid her sin and failure...
      He loved her and forgave her
        again.
   she found enough love to start over.

"a loving church still cared.
they forgave her, too.
   i don't know where that church was, but
      Jesus must have been proud. a lot
of churches today, i'm afraid, would
      have lost faith in marla, and deserted her.

"this time, marla knew she must give her baby up.
somewhere in the world today that baby girl
is now growing up in a loving home...
   somewhere where marla will never see her again
      until heaven.
   and there must be many who understand that
      same lifelong pain, that somewhere your

flesh and blood lives and moves apart
from you.

"but today, marla is married to a man
who loves marla in spite of her past.
he trusts her and believes in her and forgives
her just as Jesus has...
God has given them several more children,
and their home is Christ-centered.

"you see,
it does seem incredible...
but that is how deep and how high and how wide
God's love is.

"scars remain...
yes.
we reap what we sow...
yes.
but sins are forgiven.
marla is WHOLE
a fresh, new life is hers."[10]

And that's the Barnabas style — encouragement, generosity, forgiveness, a second chance. "Blue-collar Christianity" — the compassionate touch, hope for a hurting world.

Footnotes

1. Fred Smith, *You and Your Network* (Waco: Word Books Publisher, 1984).

2. J. Wallace Hamilton, *Where Now Is Thy God?* (Old Tappan: Fleming H. Revell Company, 1969) p. 61.

3. Norman Cousins, *Saturday Review*.

4. Donald MacLeod, "Something Happened in Church," quoted in *The Twentieth Century Pulpit*, edited by James W. Cox (Nashville: Abingdon Press, 1978) p. 134.

5. John L. Gwaltney, "Miz Mabel's Legacy" (*Reader's Digest*, Jan. 1982) pp. 118, 116.

6. Ibid., p. 119.

7. Ibid., p. 118.

8. Ibid., p. 116.

9. Norman Cousins, *Human Options*, quoted in *Disciplines for the Inner Life*, by Bob Benson and Michael W. Benson (Waco: Word Books Publisher, 1985) p. 310.

10. Ann Kiemel, *It's Incredible* (Wheaton: Tyndale House Publishers, Inc., 1977) pp. 80-84.

Chapter 3

FAILURE ISN'T FINAL

Lord,
here's my life,
such as it is,
a patchwork of small successes
interlaced with innumerable failures.
An ordinary life, for the most part,
used and sometimes misused,
definitely in need of new management.
Govern me, I pray, with Your holy love.
Direct all the decisions of my life.
Teach me to budget
my limited resources of time and talent,
lest I continue to squander them foolishly
on selfish goals
and things that don't really matter.

I've mismanaged it for so long,
made so many mistakes,
    wasted so many opportunities,
       failed so frequently —
that now I wonder
if even You can balance the books.
I take hope when I remember
    David,
       Jacob,
          Peter,
            even John Mark.

Failures every one,
yet You redeemed their mistakes,
used their failures
as tools in Your hands,
made even their willfulness and wanderings
to contribute to Your eternal design.

Then there's the prodigal
who insisted on doing it his way,
and ended up feeding swine in the far country.
He too came back,
was forgiven and restored.
His failures forgotten!

Today
I am that prodigal,
a failure through and through.
But I'm coming back to You,
    somewhat the worse for wear,
        maybe even broken in places.
Hoping that once again You'll be the forgiving Father.
    Knowing that if anyone
    can balance the books,
    can redeem my failures
    and make the old me new again,
    it's You!

Do it, Lord, I pray.
Amen.

Chapter 3

FAILURE ISN'T FINAL

Failure hurts! It's disappointing, embarrassing, humiliating. Say everything you want to about its benefits, say it builds character, say it teaches us compassion; it still hurts. That is not to say that the benefits are not real, for they are. Failure can contribute significantly to personal development, but that does not nullify the pain. It redeems it, gives it a noble purpose, but it does not eliminate it. Any way you cut it, failure hurts!

One of my most vivid memories of failure concerns a disappointment which I suffered several years ago. Brenda and I had offered ourselves as candidates for the pastorate of a promising church. When the congregation voted, they elected someone else.

Even now I can remember the rush of heat that rose to my face when the chairman of the pulpit committee telephoned to tell me the church's decision. I had taken the call in the bedroom, at my desk. Now I had to return to the living room to face Brenda and some special friends who were eagerly awaiting the news. Why, I wondered, had I invited them to spend the evening with us?

Earlier, when I was sure we would be elected, it had seemed like a good idea, a relaxing way to pass the time while we waited for the chairman's telephone call. Now I had to face them, I had to tell them that the congregation had voted to call the other minister: What could I say? How could I explain it?

For several minutes more I lingered in the bedroom, pretending to be on the phone, delaying the inevitable moment as long as possible. A host of emotions swept over me. Embarrassment — I felt diminished somehow, like a reject. The church had judged me, my ministry, and I had been found wanting. Anger boiled inside of me: What a stupid way to select a pastor. I felt helpless, as if someone else was in control of my life, and all the more angry because I was powerless to do anything about it. The bitter taste of disappointment filled my mouth. I had been so sure that this church was right for us, so sure they would elect us as their pastors. All of our plans had been based on that assurance, and now we were left with nothing.

When finally I returned to the living room, I didn't have to say anything, my face said it all. I couldn't bring myself to speak. I didn't know what to say. Besides, I couldn't trust my voice.

After a silence that seemed to last forever, Brenda said ever so softly, "We didn't get it, did we?"

I managed a nod, nothing more. Thankfully, our friends had the grace to share our disappointment silently without offering a false comfort.

That was fourteen years ago, and since then I've experienced a number of additional failures. After one year as associate pastor, I was asked to resign. A church I was pastoring suffered a painful split. Three book manuscripts I submitted for publication were rejected repeatedly and have never been published. I made a terrible mistake when I hired my first associate minister and, after only one year, I had to ask him to resign. There's more, but I think I've made my point.

Am I a failure? Hardly, but I have failed a number of times. And I guess that's the first lesson we must learn if we are to overcome our failures. Remember, failing doesn't make us a failure. Giving up, accepting our failure, refusing to try again, does!

When we see successful people, we often assume that they "got all the breaks," that they were always in the right place at the right time, that they've never failed, never been rejected. If the truth were known, very few people accomplish anything worthwhile the first time they attempt it. In fact, even the most successful people generally have a checkerboard career of both success and failure.

Consider Winston Churchill: "During the Boer War he was jailed in Pretoria, South Africa, but later escaped. Years passed and as first Lord of the Admiralty, he was personally blamed for the costly Dardanelles disaster and forced to resign. Even after successfully steering his country through another war, his countrymen rejected him at the polls. Yet he remained undaunted and rose again to be the Prime Minister of England in her darkest hour. He died the most esteemed man of his generation."[1]

"For more than twenty years Robert Frost was a failure. He often said that during this time he was one of the very few persons who knew he was a poet. The world mourned his recent passing, and today he towers as one of America's greatest verse writers. His poems have been published in twenty-two languages, with his American edition alone selling over a record million copies. He was a four time winner of the coveted Pulitzer Prize for poetry and had more honorary degrees thrust upon him than probably any other man of letters."[2]

For years Alexander Graham Bell was a failure, at least he suffered one humiliating setback after another. He spent much of his life being laughed at and ridiculed as he crisscrossed New England trying to raise venture capital for the production of his invention. Today nobody laughs at Bell. But he had to overcome failure in order to succeed.

When Walt Disney went around Hollywood with his little "Steamboat Willie" cartoon idea, he was bankrupt and, by all normal standards, a failure.

Johnny Carson's first effort at his own network show was a terrible flop and for years he was a forgotten man, but he didn't give up. Today he is the standard by which all TV personalities are judged.

That's all well and good — encouraging, in fact — but it also raises some questions: Why does failure destroy some people but not others? Are there any principles for overcoming failure? And how can I turn my mistakes, my defeats, into successes?

These are not just theoretical questions either, but life-and-death issues for those of us who have wrestled with obvious shortcomings. A number of times over the past twenty years I have found myself mired in failure, tempted to despair, to give up. Yet each time I found God faithful and, in His grace, resources which enabled me to overcome. He did not supernaturally deliver me; rather, He gave me insights and understandings which enabled me to work through my failures and at the same time prepared me to deal with future difficulties.

The scriptures have been enormously helpful to me. From them I have learned that God can redeem our mistakes; that is, cause them to contribute to our ultimate Christlikeness. Which is not to say that God wills them, only that He will use them if we let Him. Romans 8:28 (KJV) says, "...all things work together for good to them that love God...." And that includes our mistakes, even our failures!

Numerous biblical examples have convinced me that failure is not final; at least, it need not be. Nowhere is this truth more clearly demonstrated than in the experience of Moses. At forty, in a fit of temper (righteous indignation, it might be argued), Moses killed an Egyptian taskmaster and buried his body in the sand. When the authorities got wind of it, Moses fled to the backside of the desert where he spent the next forty years as a fugitive, herding sheep.

Think of it — from a prince in Pharaoh's palace to a fugitive on the backside of the desert. And even that wasn't the half of it, for it does not so much as hint at the spiritual and psychological repercussions. To understand them, we must compare Stephen's account in Acts 7 with Moses' own writing in Exodus. Stephen describes Moses as "... powerful in speech and action" (Acts 7:22). Yet Moses writes, "...I am not eloquent...I am slow of speech, and of a slow tongue (Ex. 4:10 KJV). In *The Living Bible*, he says, "...I have a speech impediment."

Initially this may seem like a contradiction, but upon closer examination it simply reveals the devastating effect of Moses' failure. Before that fateful day, he was confident, self-assured and a gifted speaker. Already he had accepted God's call to deliver His people. Acts 7:25 says, "Moses thought that his own people would realize that God was using him to rescue them, but they did not." After killing the Egyptian, he was full of self-doubt. If he was really called of God, why did he fail? Why did his own people reject him? Was his call just a figment of his imagination?

Then there's the loss of status and social prestige with the accompanying psychological consequences. From Pharaoh's palace to a sheepherder's tent. From the urbane splendor of Egypt to the desolate wilderness of Midian. No wonder Moses stuttered. His self-esteem was shattered. Guilt trampled him, left him tongue-tied. Regret rendered him mute. For forty years he was a forgotten man, a failure. Then God spoke to him out of a burning bush.

Imagine, if you can, an eighty-year-old man — a dark, weather-beaten sheepherder — standing barefoot by a burning bush in the middle of the desert, hiding his face in his hands like a modest maiden. That's Moses. He is barefoot because the voice out of the midst of the bush told him he was treading on holy ground and bare feet were in order. Hiding his face was his own idea, and a good one, for what man among us dares to look the Almighty in the eye?

In moments like that, when it's just you and God and nobody else, every selfish act, every disobedience, every failure returns with shameful clarity. And yet God did not chasten Moses, did not chide him. Instead He renewed his call, "...I am sending you to Pharaoh to bring my people the Israelites out of Egypt" (Ex. 3:10).

"But Moses said to God, 'Who am I, that I should go...?' " (v. 11). Which was his way of saying, "Don't You remember who I am? I'm a wanted man, a murderer. Forty years ago I tried and I failed. They didn't believe me then, why should they believe me now? I'm flattered, God, but You've got the wrong man. I'm not qualified."

He was right, as far as he went; but he missed the point. God's call is not so much the confirmation of our gifts and qualifications as it is the promise of His sufficiency. His call is a sovereign act of His grace and faithfulness.

Now here's the good news, especially to those of us who are struggling with failure. Moses overcame his past failure, or perhaps I should say, God redeemed it. Not only did he get another chance, but this time he succeeded. He challenged Egypt's military might and won; he confronted Pharaoh and negotiated the release of two million slaves, and then led them to freedom. Subsequently he gave them a system of government, a theocracy. He organized their religion, designed and built their place of worship, and defined God for them. For forty years, he was their spiritual father, their priest, their prophet, their general and their prime minister. In addition, he penned the first five books of the Bible, including the Ten Commandments which, to this day, are the foundation for moral order in our society.

If you've failed, don't despair, not even if you've made a real mess of your life. Paul says, "...God's gifts and his call are irrevocable" (Rom. 11:29). That is to say, there is nothing you can do, no willful disobedience, no foolish mistake, which will cause God to revoke His call on your life.

Or as James S. Stewart, the Scottish preacher, says: "There is nothing in heaven or earth so dogged and determined and stubborn and persistent as the grace (of God) that wills to save!...For you see, it means that to the person who believes in God there is no such thing as an irreparable disaster, no discord that cannot contribute to the final harmony, no thorns that cannot be woven into a crown, no breakaway from the original pattern that cannot itself be wrought in by God's skillful fingers to a new completed design."[3]

That means there is no failure God cannot redeem!

This truth was driven home to me about five years ago when I found myself in a painful mess, mostly of my own making. I had invited a friend to join the pastoral staff of my church and after just a few weeks I realized I had made a terrible mistake. We both tried hard to make it work, but in spite of our best efforts things continued to deteriorate. After ten months I knew something had to be done. Reluctantly I decided to ask for his resignation. It was perhaps the most difficult decision of my life.

The fateful morning arrived and I invited him into my office. With a sense of despair I informed him of my decision. I tried to make it as painless as possible, but such a painful thing cannot be done painlessly. The church board had agreed on a generous severance package, including four months' pay, and a love offering from the congregation, as well as a reception in his honor. Still, all he heard was my rejection and for the first twenty minutes he gave vent to his hurt and frustration.

I listened without saying anything, without making any attempt to defend myself or to justify my decision. I had already detailed my reason and there was nothing more I could do. No matter what I might say, he was still going to misunderstand, still going to blame me.

To fully understand my failure and my pain, you must remember that this man was a close friend. I wasn't simply terminating a staff member, I was asking a dear friend to resign. It was more like a divorce. We had been friends for ten years, and I knew this might well mean the end of our friendship. Not that I wanted it to end, I just recognized that painful fact. After he left, I sat at my desk for a long time and wept silently.

The days that followed were very similar to those experienced by the grieving family when a loved one dies. Duties were carried out by rote, obligations fulfilled, tasks completed, but it was like sleep walking. And the hurt never went away.

I blamed myself, not for his resignation, but for the mistake of hiring him in the first place. If only I had heeded the unspoken reservations of the official church board. If only I had sought the counsel of my spiritual mentor. If only I had listened to Brenda's concerns. But no, I had to do it my way. And now look what I had done. Not only had I lost a friend, I had shamed him as well, wounded his spirit, and caused my congregation no little pain — to say nothing of the wordless grief deep inside of me, terrible, and more real than can ever be imagined.

Like children whose parents suddenly announce that they are divorcing, the congregation felt hurt and confused. They loved us both, and yet they were being forced to make a choice between us. Not that we wanted them to do so, but that's simply the nature of the thing. They observed our politeness in public and could not help but compare it to the comfortable camaraderie we had exhibited initially. Our pain and brokenness became theirs, and a somberness settled over our fellowship.

His resignation wasn't effective for three weeks, and he continued to come into the office almost daily, although there was really no reason for it. After the first day there were no more outbursts, just an unnatural politeness. We spoke to each other, carefully lest we inflict some new pain, and our guardedness was more painful than anything we might have said. We made small talk, tried to pretend everything was as it should be, but there was a deadness in our voices, a tragic reminder of the terrible thing that had happened, a thing from which our friendship might never recover.

Those three weeks were the longest of my entire life. It seemed they would never end, but finally the reception was over and he moved out of the office. Still my grief remained, hung over me like fog blanketing the land. Depression made me lethargic, fed my self-doubt, haunted me with painful questions. Perhaps this was the "Peter Principle" in practice — maybe I was living proof that people tend to rise to the level of their incompetence. Maybe I wasn't capable of pastoring a church with a multiple staff.

His criticism returned with a vengeance — I was insecure, I was two-faced, I was jealous, I wasn't capable of an honest relationship. Maybe he was right. Maybe it was all my fault. If only I could go back and do it all again. If only. . . .

My painful thoughts triggered something deep inside me and a vague memory came to mind, a kind of half-formed thought, something I had maybe heard someone say. Concentrating, I tried to bring it into focus, but it eluded me, sat just out of reach on the edge of my mind.

Regret again: *If only*. . . . That was it!

I remembered having heard a noted psychologist say that the two saddest words in the human vocabulary are "if only." He went on to explain that many people feel trapped in their failures and spend a lifetime saying. "if only": If only I had tried harder. If only I had been a better parent. If only I hadn't been unfaithful. If only. . . .

To avoid this kind of self-imposed bondage, he suggested that we substitute the words "next time": Next time I will use better judgment. Next time I will be a better parent, a better husband. Next time I will try harder.

"If only" focuses on past failures and sentences us to a lifetime of regret. "Next time" turns our attention to the future and inspires us to try again.

With real determination I turned my attention to the future. I made up my mind, then and there, that I wasn't going to live the rest of my life imprisoned by that one failure. I would learn from it, to be sure, and I would do my best to never make the same mistakes again, but there was nothing to be gained by continually berating myself. Regret was a luxury I could not long afford.

Another story came to mind, this one about Mr. Watson, President of International Business Machines. Once, so the story goes, he gave a struggling writer some invaluable advice:

"You're making a common mistake. You're thinking of failure as the enemy of success. But it isn't that at all. Failure is a teacher — a harsh one, perhaps, but the best. You say you have a desk full of rejected manuscripts? That's great! Every one of those manuscripts was rejected for a reason. Have you pulled them to pieces looking for that reason? That's what I have to do when an idea backfires or a sales program fails. You've got to put failure to work for you.

"You can be discouraged by failure — or you can learn from it. So go ahead and make mistakes. Make all you can. Because, remember, that's where you'll find success. On the far side of failure."[4]

How had he put it? "Failure is a teacher — a harsh one, perhaps, but the best."[5] Not an enemy, but a teacher. "You can be discouraged by failure," he had said, "or you can learn from it."[6]

What a thought! I could learn from this tragic experience. It need not destroy me. This pain, this awful, unrelenting pain, could be made an ally. Yes, she was a harsh teacher, but her very harshness sensitized me to lessons I might otherwise have never learned.

With great tenderness I embraced my pain, invited it in, made peace with it. It did not go away then, nor for a long time thereafter, but, at least, it was no longer pointless. Now it had a purpose, and that made it somehow more bearable. I resolved that I would not waste that failure. It had cost me dearly, and I was determined to learn everything I could from it.

Carefully I examined the entire episode. Step by step I went over it, beginning with the initial idea and working toward its tragic end. I catalogued my mistakes, then I dissected them looking for erroneous logic, improper motives, inaccurate conclusions, even relational failures. And I found them too. They were there where I never thought they would be. This too was painful, for I was seeing myself as I had never seen me before, but I strengthened myself with the knowledge that God was redeeming my failures. He would use each painful lesson to make me a more effective pastor, a more compassionate person.

One final thing remained unfinished, and I had to decide what I was going to do about it. My congregation was still troubled, unanswered questions remained, my credibility was suspect. After extended prayer, I decided to confess my failures publicly, own my mistakes, and seek the forgiveness of those I had wronged. The church knew that something had gone wrong, knew that somewhere I had made some mistakes. What they didn't know was whether I realized my mistakes, and this more than anything else was the source of their uncertainty. Since that time, I've come to understand that people will forgive us almost any mistake if we recognize and acknowledge it. What they can't forgive is our unwillingness to admit our failure.

As I think about that whole experience now, five years later, I realize that as painful as it was, it was an invaluable learning experience for me. God did not cause that failure, nor did He will it — that was my own doing, and I will take full responsibility for it — but He truly used it.

Perhaps you're thinking: That's all well and good, but my failures are of a more serious kind. Thus far you've not even touched upon them. All you've written about are business failures, or ventures which went sour. Painful, to be sure, but not sinful, definitely not sinful. My failures are of a spiritual nature. I've failed my family and my God. Is there any hope for me?

Some years ago, a man came to my office for counseling. He chose to see me rather than his own pastor, so great was his shame. He had done a despicable thing, and now he couldn't live with himself. Hardly had I closed the office door before he fell to his knees sobbing. For several minutes he wept before the Lord. Finally he was able to compose himself and only then did he share his dark secret.

He was a good man, a Christian, and he had never intended to become involved in sin, but he had. It had started innocently enough with morning coffee at a nearby convenience store. Then he started browsing through the pornographic magazines on the counter while he drank his coffee. Then he purchased one, then another.

From that point, the story has an all too familiar progression. From magazines he went to x-rated videos, and then he secured the services of a prostitute. Of course, this degenerating progression didn't happen overnight. It took place over a period of months and with each step he told himself he would go no farther, but he seemed powerless to stop.

He lived in a self-made hell. There were moments of lustful pleasure, to be sure, but they were followed by hours of shame, days and weeks of unspeakable regret. Yet even in his shame he was irresistibly drawn toward the very thing he hated. His desperate prayers seemed powerless against the demons within. Now he lived in secrecy and fear. What if someone saw him? What if his wife or someone from his church found out? His marriage suffered, as did his church life. He wanted out, he wanted to stop, but something seemed to drive him on.

Then his worst fears were realized. He contacted a sexually transmitted disease and infected his wife with it. Thankfully it wasn't AIDS, but it still meant that he had to tell her so she could receive treatment. What was going to happen now? Would she forgive him? Could she ever trust him again? How foolish, how insane, his sins now seemed.

After hearing him out, I helped him identify his failures and the steps necessary to rectify them. He had failed God, sinned against Him, and now he needed forgiveness and restoration. He had failed his wife, been unfaithful to her, broken their wedding vows, and now he had to acknowledge his sins against their marriage and seek her forgiveness as well. And he had sinned against himself, betrayed his own values, dishonored everything he had once held sacred and dear.

Overcoming a failure of that nature, that magnitude, isn't easy, and he spent months battling guilt and depression. He couldn't forgive himself, so why should he believe that God would forgive him? He wanted to believe, but he didn't dare. Forgiveness seemed too good to be true. Yet he couldn't live with the condemnation either. It drove him to despair, told him it was no use, that he would never be any different. And it became a birthing place for temptation. If he was never again to know the joy of his salvation, then why not plunge headlong into the pleasures of sin?

We battled those monsters together, using both prayer and the Word of God. First we reviewed what the scriptures taught about forgiveness. That it is always God's will to forgive, that He is faithful, that He will not give up on us. He memorized 1 John 1:9: "If we confess our sins, he is faithful and just and will forgive us our sins and purify us from all unrighteousness."

Then we dealt with condemnation and I helped him differentiate between the conviction of the Holy Spirit and the condemnation of the enemy. Second Corinthians 7:10 says, "Godly sorrow [conviction] brings repentance that leads to salvation and leaves no regret, but worldly sorrow [condemnation] brings death."

Holy Spirit conviction makes us painfully aware of our sinfulness and our failures, but even as it does, we are motivated to confess our sins and try again. We hear ourselves saying, "I know I've failed, but I will do better next time." Condemnation, on the other hand, makes us feel like giving up. It tells us that we will never be any different, that God is sick of our repeated failures and ready to wash His hands of us. It drives us into hiding, away from God.

The Holy Spirit is always very specific when He convicts us of sin. He puts His finger on it, identifies it, so we can deal with it, bring it to God and get rid of it. Condemnation is vague, general; it leaves us feeling guilty, unworthy, but not really sure why. It does not identify a particular sin, lest we deal with it and be delivered. In fact, the only time condemnation is specific is when it condemns us of sins we've already confessed.

Remember, if you are feeling guilty about a sin which you've already confessed, that feeling is not from God, so reject it. When God forgives our sins, He is done with them; He never brings them up to us again: ". . .as far as the east is from the west, so far has he removed our transgressions from us" (Ps. 103:12).

Then the man and I had to deal with his temptation. There were certain things he couldn't do, certain places he couldn't go, not because they were sinful in themselves, but because of his propensity to sin. For instance, he could not go into a convenience store, the risk was simply too great. Nor could he go in any place that rented videos. Extreme? Perhaps, but we were dealing with matters of life and death: "If your right eye causes you to sin, gouge it out and throw it away. It is better for you to lose one part of your body than for your whole body to be thrown into hell" (Matt. 5:29).

And there was his marriage. His wife was shattered. This wasn't the man she had married. That man was good and godly, incapable of the kind of things this man had done. Unspeakable things, evil acts beyond the realm of her understanding. And not only had he done them, confessed in sordid detail, but she carried in her own body the evil evidence. She had trusted him, never thought to question his late hours. She had believed him when he told her his preoccupation was job-related pressure. But now her trust was gone, crushed beneath the awful fact of his unfaithfulness.

Yet she wanted this marriage to work, wanted to forgive him as badly as he wanted to be forgiven, but could she? Could she get rid of her hurt and anger without destroying him, them? Could she learn to trust him again, respect him as a godly man, as the spiritual leader in their home? These and a hundred more questions haunted her every waking moment.

Together we processed them. The three of us worked our way through them, painfully, one at a time, and bit by bit their lives began to come together again. It was slow, and it was hard. There were several crises, moments when it didn't look as though we were going to make it, but by God's grace we did.

That was many years ago, and I'm thankful I can tell you that God's grace was sufficient for that man, for both of them. The road back was painful and long, requiring months of marital counseling and intense personal ministry, but it was well worth it. Today they are happily married and active in their church.

And this is not an isolated incident either. God has a long history of redeeming our failures, turning our worst blunders into opportunities for personal growth and spiritual development. Whatever your failures, you need not despair. With God's help, you can not only overcome them, but you can learn from them as well; you can turn a painful disappointment into a positive growth experience.

"You can be discouraged by failure — or you can learn from it. So go ahead and make mistakes. Make all you can. Because, remember, that's where you'll find success. On the far side of failure."[7]

79

Don't live in the past. Learn from it, but don't become a prisoner of it. "Finish each day," said Ralph Waldo Emerson, "and be done with it. You have done what you could. Some blunders and absurdities no doubt crept in; forget them as soon as you can. Tomorrow is a new day; begin it well and serenely. . . ."[8]

Christianity is a gospel of new beginnings, second chances. God is a "next time" God, and He calls us to be "next time" people: "Brothers, if someone is caught in a sin, you who are spiritual should restore him gently. . ." (Gal. 6:1).

Footnotes:

1. Charles Hembree, *Pocket of Pebbles* (Grand Rapids: Baker Book House, 1969), p. 36.

2. Ibid., p. 53.

3. James S. Stewart, *The Wind of the Spirit* (Nashville: Abingdon Press, 1968), pp. 143, 145.

4. Arthur Gordon, *A Touch of Wonder* (Old Tappan: Fleming H. Revell Company, 1974), p. 73.

5. Ibid., p. 73.

6. Ibid., p. 73.

7. Ibid., p. 73.

8. Ralph Waldo Emerson, quoted in *Dawnings, Finding God's Light in the Darkness,* edited by Phyllis Hobe (New York: Guideposts Associates, Inc., 1981), p. 154.

Chapter 4

WHEN THE VOW BREAKS

It was 1 a.m.
and the ringing of the bedside extension
jarred me out of an exhausted sleep.
The voice on the other end of the line
sounded desperate.

My initial reaction was resentment
(the "old man" is not dead yet),
then amazement — how did she get my number?
At first I couldn't remember her:
    Nancy —
        from Craig, Colorado?

But as she continued to talk,
bits and pieces started coming together.
A desperate prayer
as she had lain in a hospital bed facing death.
A miracle of healing —
    kidney failure reversed,
        sugar diabetes totally healed.
Praise the Lord!

Now she was desperate again.
Her husband of fifteen years
had walked out,
leaving her alone and broke,
facing fifty without a hope in the world.

Suicide wooed her
with false promises of sweet oblivion.
In her darkest hour
she grabbed her Bible
and a picture of Brenda and me fell out.

A tiny hope sprang to life:
    "God used Richard once to save my life,
    maybe He will use him again."
A desperate prayer for guidance.

She had moved from Craig before we did.
Try as she might, she couldn't remember
where we now lived.
Another desperate cry for help.

Houston came to mind,
so she dialed Directory Assistance.
She reached my parents who gave her my unlisted number,
and now in the dark of night we made contact.
By this time all the exhausted resentment was gone,
    as was the confusion.
        replaced by His compassion,
            and a sense that this call was no accident.

Faith was born anew,
prayer was offered,
Jesus came!

Only time will reveal the full answer,
but her hope was restored.
Thanks, Lord, for letting me
be Your voice of love and healing
to a desperate woman
in the dark of night.

Chapter 4

WHEN THE VOW BREAKS

Recently I found myself face to face with a desperate young woman. I was standing in the altar area at the front of the church, following the benediction, when she introduced herself. Immediately she began pouring out her heart to me. In a matter of minutes she had given me the "run down" on her third marriage, the pertinent details anyway, at least from her perspective.

She was just four months into the marriage and already it was showing signs of failure. She had married "on the rebound," out of loneliness, to a man she hardly knew, and now a third divorce seemed likely.

It was her husband's first marriage, and much to his chagrin he had soon discovered that a wife was far more demanding than he ever could have imagined. She invaded his privacy, talked when he sought only silence, demanded his attention when he simply wanted to be left alone with his thoughts. He was an engineer, a man at home with intellectual abstractions, a loner married to his career. To him sex was okay from time to time; that is, as long as it didn't interfere with some project he was working on, or if he wasn't too tired. But sleeping together was out of the question.

He needed his rest, and he couldn't get comfortable with *her* in his bed. Needless to say, his eccentricities only aggravated her insecurities.

Two previous divorces had left her lonely and unsure of herself, with an insatiable need for love and attention — a need which threatened to consume her new husband. She wanted, no demanded, every spare minute of his time. He was her only friend, her sole source of human companionship. She couldn't bear to let him out of her sight, talked incessantly, clung to him until he couldn't take any more. When he withdrew, as he must from time to time in order to survive, she sensed his distance and felt threatened, which only increased her desperation, causing her to cling that much tighter.

Now, too late, she realized her mistake. Emotionally she wasn't ready to remarry. The wounds from her two previous marriages were far from healed, leaving her less than whole, unfit for marriage. Because she rushed the relationship, she married a man she hardly knew, a stranger really, and now she was living with the consequences. Without some major adjustments, this marriage too seemed doomed to failure.

An isolated incident? Hardly.

"According to *U.S. News and World Report,* marriages are being dissolved at the rate of one every twenty-seven seconds. The numbers exceed one million every year, more than twice the divorces of two decades ago."[1]

Think of it: two million people each year shattered by divorce! And that figure does not take into account the number of children involved. Statistics now indicate that forty-five percent of the children currently growing up in the United States will be the victims of their parents' separation or divorce.[2] Add to that the divorced couple's parents, their brothers and sisters, plus their close friends, and several more million lives are affected by the trauma of divorce.

The effect of divorce can be compared to that of a rock thrown into the center of a placid pond. The biggest splash is at the point of impact, but the ripples go out in an ever-expanding circle. When a marriage ends, no one hurts like the husband and wife, yet the pain of divorce doesn't stop with them. If there are children involved, they often feel that they are somehow to blame. Or they feel as if they have been divorced, that their father or mother no longer loves them.

Then there's the pain experienced by the divorced person's parents. A pain often complicated by guilt: Where did I go wrong? Surely this divorce would not have happened if I had been a better parent.

Add to this the increased financial burden which is often placed on them, plus the inevitable emotional strain, and you get a glimpse of divorce from their perspective. Frequently, they become a "dumping ground" for their divorced children's emotional baggage as well. Believe me, they suffer too — financially and emotionally.

And what about the divorced couple's friends? If they were close, if they cared deeply, then they too will find themselves hurting. Even if they are able to remain friends with both parties, they have been divorced from the couple. They have lost something precious — a meaningful relationship. Chances are that one party or the other, perhaps both parties, will try to use them as a sounding board, making neutrality virtually impossible. They may even try to poison their friends against their former spouse. As a result, few friendships ever really survive a divorce.

For the divorced person himself, the pain can seem unending. Most counselors agree that it takes at least two years for a man to recover from a divorce, usually three years for a woman. Few things in life are more devastating to a person's sense of self-worth. He feels that he has failed at the most important relationship in his life, and he is literally being torn apart on the inside. If he is a Christian, then he must also contend with the question of how this affects his relationship with God.

And, speaking of God, many divorced persons harbor anger toward Him, howbeit unacknowledged: Why didn't God answer my prayers? Why didn't He save my marriage? Then they feel guilty for those "unacceptable" feelings too.

According to psychologist Dr. Gary Collins, "Divorce is accompanied by an almost endless range of emotions, including: anxiety, guilt, fear, sadness, depression (sometimes accompanied by thoughts of suicide), anger, bitterness and frustration. Often along with the distress, there is a sense of euphoria and relief but this sometimes stimulates more guilt. Most couples experience periods of indecision, confusion or vacillation and sometimes there is hyperalertness, as if the person is waiting expectantly for something else to go wrong. The body, of course, cannot maintain a continuing state of tension and vigilance, so often psychosomatic illnesses result."[3]

It is impossible to minister effectively to the divorced without understanding something of the trauma they experience. Yet far too often the Church's approach has been theological rather than relational. Most discussions of divorce from a Christian perspective focus on questions like: Is it ever right to divorce? Or, can a divorced person ever remarry without living in adultery? If so, to whom and under what circumstances?

Other discussions concentrate on the "why" questions: Why are so many couples divorcing? Why doesn't the Church do something about divorce?

These are important issues, to be sure — critical issues, in fact — and they must be addressed. But if that is as far as we go, we will fall short of actually ministering healing and restoration to those suffering from the consequences of divorce.

Many believers have difficulty honestly facing the issue of ministry to the divorced. There are probably a number of reasons for this, but the two most obvious are: 1) there seems to be a fear that acceptance of the divorced person will be misunderstood as approval of divorce, that if we do anything to ease the painfulness of divorce we might somehow encourage others to seek the termination of their marriages as well; and 2) the Church's widespread ignorance regarding the tragedy of divorce. If a person has never gone through a divorce, it is hard for him to appreciate the sense of loss and personal failure, the fear and confusion, and, of course, the inevitable guilt. As a consequence, the divorced person is often required to walk through his valley of the shadow of death alone. Or, he can seek the company of other divorced persons, mostly unbelievers. Yet, in their unbelief, they are often more "Christian" than the less compassionate Christians themselves.

It's impossible to comprehend the magnitude of the tragedy of divorce without some grasp of the miracle of marriage. It's not a miracle in the sense that it happens supernaturally without effort or investment on our part. Rather marriage is a miracle in the sense that in spite of our immaturity and selfishness, in spite of our independence and differing personalities, we truly become one, at least for a time. And having experienced that blessed oneness, for however fleeting a time, we can never be satisfied with anything less.

Another name for that blessed oneness is companionship, intimacy. To the casual observer, such intimacy, such blessed oneness, may appear optional. Nice, but not necessary. Not so. Having once experienced it, now we can't live without it. We may exist without it, even as we can exist without love, but we can't truly live without it.

In *As For Me And My House*, Walter Wangerin, Jr., writes: "Listen: particular and loving relationships are more than merely 'good'; they are an essential quality of life. They affirm the individual's being. They assure him that he is. They both support him physically and define him spiritually. They give him a special place in the world, and they acknowledge the good purpose of his presence in that place. It is more than comfort we receive from other people: it is identity, so I know who I am. It is being itself, and the conviction of personal worth."[4]

This is particularly true of marriage. As Wangerin said: "(It) gives him a special place in the world, and (it) acknowledges the good purpose of his presence in that place."[5]

He then gives a simple description of how that works in his own marriage:

"...there are times when Thanne and I lie abed at night, nearing sleep. Almost we float apart from one another; sleep is so private an activity, and darkness seems to close us into ourselves. But then Thanne whispers, waking me: 'Wally? Wally?' And suddenly the fact that she has called my name — that she knows my name and can say it, that she whispers it in the trust that I will hear her — makes me to know me. Her voice, her word, her presence startles me with the knowledge of selfhood. I distinctly realize, in the tingling darkness, that I am. Moreover I am not lost; I am not elsewhere or lonely or slipping into unreality, or else dead. No, I'm right here, in bed beside her, in this special place, enveloped in her sleepy love. Oh, that is a marvelous feeling — of being: an unspeakable gift of God."[6]

That's it. Marriage is an unspeakable gift of God! We enter marriage with such bright expectations, and well we should. Parents shed bittersweet tears of painful happiness. Friends laugh, hug our necks and congratulate us. It's a special moment, holy and happy. We have vowed our faithfulness "til death do us part." We belong to each other as we have never belonged to anyone before. We relate to one another in a way no one else can ever relate to either of us, or we to them. She is my only wife. I am her only husband.

In all of our other relationships, we are one among many. One child among several children in our family, one friend among many friends, one student among many students, one of many players on the team, one of several employees on the job, one of many.... Not now, not here! For the first time ever, I am the only one to her, and she is the only one to me. Truly an unspeakable gift!

That doesn't mean, though, that we have a fairy-tale existence of living "happily ever after." In reality, marriage is both a gift and a discipline. God gives us each other and the tools for cultivating our blessed oneness, but it is up to us to work the soil of our relationship all the days of our lives.

There will be the inevitable conflicts, little hurts and not so little hurts, bitter quarrels and haunting fears. Pressures too, which pull at us, causing us to drift apart. Silence beneath our words, and loneliness which only those who have known the blessed oneness can imagine. Holy moments too when forgiveness gives birth to intimacy, when the silences and the separation are put behind us, and once again we know who we are and where we belong.

In truth, marriage is a lot like life — full of contradictions and conflicts, but for all of that still so blessed, oh so blessed. It has its moments — anniversaries and other special days, as well as unscheduled surprises and unexpected kindnesses, little gestures of love which set the heart to singing — but, for the most part, it's more pedestrian. And its those mundane details which mold the character of our relationship. Little things, which at first glance seem hardly worth mentioning. Yet as the years go by, they become daily rituals.

I mean, who ever speaks of the simple pleasure of coming home to familiar sounds — the hum of the vacuum cleaner, bath water running, conversation from the other room — yet these are the sounds of marriage. And the smells — skin cream and shampoo, clothes fresh from the dryer, furniture polish and coffee brewing. Ordinary things easily taken for granted, hardly noticed, until they are gone.

When a couple divorces, they lose all of that. Now sounds are just sounds, and smells are just smells, nothing holy or sacred about them any longer. Bath water running is just that, nothing more, and furniture polish smells sterile, antiseptic, not like love at all. No one whispers their name into the bedtime darkness, no special relationship defines them and gives them their unique place in the scheme of things. When they unconsciously fling their arm across the other side of the bed in the wee hours of the morning, there is no sleeping form, no comforting presence, to remind them that they are married — not a cold, solitary "me," but a warm, united "us."

Most marriages die slowly, more likely from ignorance and neglect than from any overt action, little by little, until there's nothing left but an empty shell. Often one or the other of the partners has seen it happening for a long time, but their pleas, and then their warnings, fell on deaf ears. Then some little thing most likely, some ordinary thing, signals the end. The youngest child graduates, he plans yet another vacation without consulting her, or she has a sudden vision of growing old together but alone. In desperation the papers are filed.

For others it comes as a total shock. "On Christmas Sunday 1980 Mona awoke to find an empty bed. Her husband was gone. She searched and called but there was no response. 'He must have gone to church early,' she thought, but he wasn't there. Time for the Christmas sermon came and there was no pastor. Search teams and police tried for days to find him without success. Not knowing if he was dead or alive, Mona became so emotionally exhausted she couldn't even find the strength to go up the stairs. For ten nights she slept on the couch while ladies from the church took turns sleeping on a mat on the floor beside her. Finally the call came. The pastor had not been kidnapped or killed; he had left Mona, the children, the church. He wouldn't tell them where he was and Mona was left in shock...."[7]

She says, "A many-sided breakdown took my pastor-husband from our house. What was to follow those first devastating hours would be days and weeks and months turning into years of heartbreak, fear, darkness, and a lot of questions. Those months were like a roller coaster — for one minute there would be hope of some reconciliation and healing only to be shattered again and back to the pits of despair. It went that way for many, many months and culminated in a divorce that I didn't want in the spring of 1982.

". . .it felt like every point, every security, everything in my life that had brought me happiness had been reduced to nothingness. I felt like someone had taken out my heart, tramped it, smashed it, beat it with a sledgehammer, and put it back inside this body. It still beats, but it beats a little crooked."[8]

No wonder many persons who have gone through a divorce conclude that they could have handled the break better if their spouse had died. At least then they would not have suffered the rejection and loss of self-worth. Loneliness yes, and loss, but the memories of their years together would still be intact, untainted. As it is, they have nothing left but the pain and a host of questions: Was it all a facade? Did he ever really love me? What things were really in his heart when we seemed so happy? Was he even then harboring secret doubts, unspoken desire?

In fact, divorce is very much like a death, with two notable differences. When a spouse dies, he or she is dead and gone. When a couple divorces, the relationship is dead, love is dead, the marriage is dead, but the spouse is still very much alive. Frequently the divorced person is required to deal with his/her ex-mate for years to come because of the children. Secondly, if a person loses a spouse through death, he or she gets sympathy and emotional support during the time of bereavement, at least initially. People feel that the surviving spouse has been dealt an unavoidable blow. Divorced persons, on the other hand, are often treated as if they are getting what they deserve. At best, they are left to find their own way — uncondemned perhaps, but ignored.

This must change. The Church cannot afford to ignore the needs of the divorced any longer. At Christian Chapel we have developed a growth group for hurting people. While it is not limited to the divorced as such, many of the participants are there because of the emotional and psychological wounds they received as a result of a marriage which failed. Some are guilt-ridden, others are angry, almost all suffer from low self-esteem. For twelve weeks they meet on Thursday nights for two hours of intense work. The spiritual and interpersonal dynamics are powerful and bit by bit these wounded people find wholeness. It's not enough, I'm sure, to meet all the needs of the divorced, but it's a beginning. And from this experience many of them become informal helpers of others just like themselves.

They are uniquely qualified to minister to the divorced because they have been there, they understand. Yet we cannot leave this ministry entirely to them, the task is far too big. The Church as a whole must support the divorced and their families, must find effective ways of facilitating their healing and their reintegration into the mainstream of life. To minister effectively, we will have to become familiar with the trauma they experience and learn how to help them cope.

Jim Smoke, former Minister to Single Adults at Garden Grove Community Church in California, conducts divorce adjustment seminars across the nation. Based on his contacts with hundreds of divorced people, he has identified three overlapping stages which they go through.[9]

The first stage is shock: This can't be happening to me. It's a bad dream. Any minute now I'll wake up and everything will be all right. It's a sick joke. Someone laugh...please.

During this stage, people react in different ways. Some withdraw, retreat into themselves, go into depression. Others can't bear to be alone. They talk incessantly, dump the details on anyone who will listen. Busyness becomes their way of coping, and they rush frantically about. As long as they don't stop, they can keep the reality of what's happening at arm's length.

One woman, whose husband divorced her after thirty-two years of marriage, writes: "I don't know how I survived those first few days and weeks after Ted left me. I wanted to die, yet I forced myself to go through the motions of living — sticking to my usual routine, teaching school two days a week. In the evenings I'd listen for the sound of Ted's car in the driveway, and then, with a sickening feeling in the pit of my stomach, I'd realize he wasn't coming home.

I kept the TV on just to hear another human voice. Alone in the empty house I cried myself into a state of numbness and exhaustion."[10]

During this stage, people often stubbornly, desperately, cling to the hope that their marriage can still be saved. In extreme cases, they refuse to give up hope even after the divorce has become final, even after their "ex" has remarried. It seems they always know of a case where a couple got back together after it appeared that all hope was gone.

Although we may realize that their life is on hold as long as they cling to that notion, it is not our place to take that hope from them. The realization of the reality of their situation must come from within, and until it does, we must continue to meet them where they are and support them with our love and our presence. Unfortunately, growth cannot occur until they honestly acknowledge the reality of their situation and take steps to deal with it.

This brings us to stage two: the adjustment stage. During this stage people begin to get in touch with their feelings. Most will experience a host of emotions ranging from rejection to anger, from guilt to self-pity, from bitterness to a sense of failure. Resist the temptation to minimize their feelings. While your efforts may provide temporary comfort, they delay the healing process. The divorced person has a lot of work to do before he can get through his negative feelings, and the sooner he gets started the better.

If he feels that he has failed, don't tell him he hasn't. In truth, he has failed, and at the most important relationship in his life — even if he did not want the divorce and did everything in his power to prevent it. The only way he can be free from that debilitating sense of failure is to accept his responsibility, own his share of the blame, and accept God's forgiveness. As long as he feels that he is only a victim and in no way responsible, he will neither seek the forgiveness of God nor receive it; thus he will continue living under a burden of repressed guilt.

Of course, the divorce is not all his fault, no matter what he did. Our ministry is to help him sort through the guilt, accepting what is rightly his and rejecting what is not. Where he has failed, he needs forgiveness; and where his spouse has failed him, he needs to be forgiving. Both acts require divine intervention; but be assured, God is faithful and He will do His part. Remember, forgiveness does not change the past, but it does unlock the future.

This adjustment stage is really a grieving period. A time when the divorced person processes his feelings. There will be moments of positive grief in which he remembers the good and the happy times in the marriage, what was and what might have been. These bittersweet times are critical to the healing process, so be patient as he relives them with you.

There will also be periods of negative grief when he seems lost in a world of self-pity. This too is a part of the healing process, and it will pass. In time he will begin to make the adjustments necessary to live life as a single person.

Remember, powerful emotions are a part of every divorce, and they can be resolved only as the divorced person works his way through them. The presence of a compassionate pastor or Christian friend can be invaluable during this time. He serves as both a nonjudgmental listener and a spiritual facilitator. He holds the divorced person accountable; he helps him deal with hurts and anger he might otherwise bury, for he knows that anger and bitterness must be acknowledged and confessed before forgiveness can be extended to the offending spouse.

True biblical confession takes place on at least two levels — fact and feeling, information and emotion. Before the divorced person can forgive his spouse for her failure, her shortcomings, he must confess his anger to God. That is, he must relive each of the hurtful incidents in the presence of God. He must describe what happened in complete and accurate detail and honestly confess his feelings; in truth, he must feel them all over again and express them completely to the Lord.

If he stops here, he has only recycled his negative emotions, but if he can move from confession to forgiveness, then healing is set in motion.

Even as he has specifically listed the hurtful incidents and the pain they caused him, so now he must specifically forgive each deed. A general forgiveness is not good enough. He was not sinned against generally but specifically, and now he must forgive in the same way, one deed at a time. To forgive someone you must let go of the hurt and anger you've held against him. This is an act of the will and it may or may not be accompanied by corresponding emotions.

When the divorced person has effectively dealt with his feelings, he moves into the last of the three stages: the growth stage.

"Here people honestly face the reality of their new status in life; set time aside for meditation, reading, prayer and personal reflection; get involved with other people, deliberately resist blaming others or themselves; fight self-pity; and seek God's guidance in making realistic plans for the future."[11]

In short, they set about the business of starting over, of rebuilding their lives. Which brings us to the question: Is there life after divorce?

Yes, but it will probably be different. You may never remarry. But that doesn't mean you can't be happy and fulfilled. One lady whose husband divorced her after thirty-two years of marriage says: "I discovered a world of possibilities — things that were out of the question while I was with Ted because he didn't approve or they didn't fit in with his work schedule. I returned to full-time teaching, for instance, and found new stimulation and pride in my job as I got involved in a class of my own.

"Most important of all, I began to see that, even when I was alone, I could still find pleasure in life. Walking, gardening, sewing — these were simple activities I'd always enjoyed on my own and there was no reason I couldn't enjoy them now. . . . Happiness is something you have to find in yourself, and that's what I'm learning to do."[12]

Then there's Shelby. Her husband divorced her, after thirteen years of marriage, when she was thirty-five. He simply moved in with another woman and left Shelby and their two children penniless. In desperation she sought and found a job, then a church where a Christian counselor helped her overcome her suicidal tendencies. With God's help she reared her children. Her daughter got a degree in business finance from San Diego State, and her son is a speech major at Point Loma College.

Shelby returned to college herself and earned a B.A. in Business Administration and a master's degree in Human Behavior. Most important of all, she has surrendered her life to God and He is using her painful experiences as a source of healing and hope for others who are going through similar trials.

She writes: "Don't waste time and energy in being bitter over the bad deal you got in life. I have lived through sexual abuse as a child, desertion and divorce as an adult. I have lived through discrimination both as a female and as a middle-aged person looking for a job. I have raised two children to be productive adults by myself. Additionally I have experienced the death of my younger sister through cancer and my own serious hospitalization with typhoid fever. Yet I believe God wants me to use all of this experience and the knowledge of his delivering power to help others. He can't do this if I'm sitting in self-pity or anger. I have learned that the acid of bitterness only eats away at the container."[13]

Think about it — Shelby was a deserted wife, a desperate woman, when God found her. Through the ministry of His Church, she found the strength to go on living, and now she is whole and has become part of that healing ministry.

In *The Communicator's Commentary #8* Maxie Dunnam refers to an incident in the novel *Other Voices, Other Rooms* where the hero is about to walk along a heavy but rotting beam over a brooding, murky creek. "Starting over,...Stepping gingerly...he felt he would never reach the other side: always he would be balanced here, suspended between land and in the dark and alone. Then feeling the board shake as Idabel started across, he remembered he had someone to be together with. And he could go on."[14]

Now that's what we're talking about, being there when the divorced person starts across that rotting beam feeling terribly alone. When he thinks he will never make it, that he will be lost forever in the darkness with his pain, then he feels the board shake as we walk with him, and he finds the strength to go on.

Footnotes

1. Ted Gest, "Divorce: How the Game Is Played Now," *U.S. News and World Report,* November 21, 1983, quoted in *Lives on the Mend* by Florence Littauer (Waco: Word Books Publisher, 1985), p. 79.

2. E. Galantly and B. Harris, *Marriage and Family Life* (Boston: Houghton Mifflin, 1982), p. 5.

3. Gary R. Collins, Ph.D., *Christian Counseling* (Waco: Word Books Publisher, 1980), p. 192.

4. Walter Wangerin, Jr., *As For Me And My House* (Nashville: Thomas Nelson Publishers, 1987), p. 58.

5. Ibid., p. 58.

6. Ibid., pp. 58,59.

7. Florence Littauer, *Lives on the Mend* (Waco: Word Books Publisher, 1985), p. 85.

8. Ibid., p. 86.

9. Quoted in *Christian Counseling* by Gary R. Collins, Ph.D. (Waco: Word Books Publisher, 1980), pp. 191,192.

10. Anonymous, "My Husband Left Me For A Younger Woman" (*Good Housekeeping*, Oct. 1983), p. 28.

11. Collins, p. 192.

12. "My Husband Left Me For A Younger Woman," p. 34.

13. Littauer, p. 102.

14. Maxie Dunnam, from *Other Voices, Other Rooms* by Truman Capote, *The Communicator's Commentary #8* (Waco: Word Book Publisher, 1982), p. 122.

Chapter 5

THE TENDER TOUCH

There's something touching about tenderness,
something that stops us in our tracks.
For just a minute
life's harsh realities are suspended,
and we catch a glimpse of life
as it could be,
     as it should be.

Tenderness is...
the touch of a mother's hand
on the fevered brow of a sick child.
It's her husband's quiet presence
in the sick room;
his strong arm around her trembling shoulder,
    his faith,
        expressed in wordless prayer.
It's a handwritten note
from one who understands,
a special scripture,
a phone call.

Tenderness is...
a shoulder to cry on
in the hour of unspeakable loss.
A friend who gives you time
    and a safe place to grieve,
who comforts
    without resorting to clichés,
who listens
    as you recount for the hundredth time
    those special memories cherished for a lifetime,
    little kindnesses taken for granted,
    endearing little habits you had never paid any
        mind to.

Tenderness is...
a friend who grieves your divorce
    without judging or rejecting you,
who includes you in holiday plans
    and family outings,
    without making you feel like a third wheel.
who listens when you need to talk
    but never pries,
    and never makes light of your pain
    with easy answers and ready-made solutions.

Tenderness is...
a compassionate believer,
    who hears your confession without seeming shocked,
    who listens with love
    as you spill every sordid detail;
    not because he needs to know,
    but because you need to talk,
        because you need to tell someone,
            because you have to tell someone.

Tenderness is...
a trusting friend
    who now knows the worst about you
    and still believes the best;
    who now says,
        "Neither do I condemn you....
        Go...sin no more...."

Tenderness is...
    all of that and more....
    life and relationships
        as God meant them to be.

Chapter 5

THE TENDER TOUCH

My introduction to the local church ministry, over twenty years ago, was a baptism by fire, or perhaps I should say by sickness and death. In the first four weeks of my pastorate, I preached three funerals and spent considerable additional time at the hospital visiting and counseling with the sick or their families.

Nothing in my training or previous experience had prepared me for this. At the hospital I was made to feel like an intruder. For the most part, the doctors tolerated my presence, or so it seemed. This was their turf, a hospital, a place where science and medicine reigned supreme. Religion and prayer, it appeared, were of little or no value.

I felt intimidated. What good could I possibly do? Of what value were scripture and prayer compared to the miracle drugs in the arsenal of modern medicine? Still, I faithfully visited the sick, and sat with their families while they were in surgery and during those critical hours when things could go either way. I did the things I had been taught to do — administer scripture and prayer — plus a lot of other things no one had ever mentioned. Like just being there and listening without saying anything, mostly because I didn't feel I had much of anything to say. Generally I felt pretty useless.

Then the strangest thing began to happen. I started receiving thank you notes from the people I had visited in the hospital. They wrote to say, "It meant so much to have you there when I was facing surgery," or, "I can't tell you how much strength I gained from your visit." I couldn't believe it. I hadn't done anything. Still it gave me more confidence the next time I made hospital calls.

About two years later I began to understand. Nine days after our daughter Leah was born, I rushed Brenda back to the hospital for emergency surgery. She was hemorrhaging, and by the time we reached the hospital, she had passed out from loss of blood. I watched as she was wheeled into surgery, and then after signing the consent forms, I was left alone with my thoughts and fears. A host of terrifying possibilities set upon me, and I paced the floor in agitation. The only comfort I found was when my mother joined me. She didn't say anything, at least nothing I can remember, but I felt better just knowing she was there. Somehow I was strengthened and encouraged by her presence.

Let a medical emergency or some other life-threatening crisis arise, and small kindnesses like an encouraging word, the touch of a hand on the shoulder, or just the presence of another person, suddenly takes on a depth of significance heretofore unimagined. Even the bravest among us, the most self-reliant, experience an inner strengthening from such human contact. The circumstances may still be just as grim, but somehow they don't seem as dark, as foreboding.

If you've never been seriously ill, or if you've never been close to someone who was, it may be difficult for you to imagine the depth of anxiety experienced in that situation. First there is the pain, constant and unrelenting, as persistent as gravity, blotting out all else, until the world is no larger than a sick room. Then there's the weakness, the inability to control one's body, to make it function on command. Now the body becomes an enemy, undermining morale, even faith.

On a psychological level, the sick person experiences a loss of power. His familiar surroundings are gone. Now he lives in an environment in which he has little or no control over his life. Before he became ill, he set his own schedule, within reasonable limits, of course. He decided when to get up and when to go to bed; what to eat, how to prepare it, and when to eat it.

Suddenly all of that is changed. He's placed in an institution where he receives the finest medical care possible, but he has lost control of his own life. He is told when to sleep, when to wake up, when to shower, and on some occasions he is even expected to relieve himself on command. He's subjected to all kinds of humiliating procedures, stripped of all modesty, poked and prodded, and experimented upon — all in the name of medicine. Eventually all of this may produce healing, but initially, at least, it is demoralizing.

Then there's the fear. Fear of the unknown: What's going to happen to me? Will I get well? Will I still be able to provide for my family, care for my children?

Mundane concerns too: Will my insurance cover the hospital bills? Do I have enough sick leave? Will I still have a job when I recover?

Interlaced with all this are the questions raised by the ever-present possibility that there may not be any recovery: Am I going to die? If so, what will become of my family? Who will look after the children?

In times of serious illness, we who are caring and compassionate Christians have at least two parties who require our love and support — the patient, and the patient's family. The ministry required of us is complex, but not complicated. It is complex in the sense that the needs are complex, multidimensional — physical, spiritual and emotional.

Perhaps these needs are best detailed by Wendy Bergren in a little pamphlet entitled "Mom Is Very Sick — Here's How to Help," which grew out of her own battle with cancer.

"Shortly after she became a mother for the third time, her doctor discovered that she had an enormous malignant tumor. In a last-ditch effort to stave off imminent death, she underwent an immediate mastectomy, hysterectomy and intensive radiation treatments. An aggressive course of chemotherapy produced every imaginable side effect and confined her to bed for two weeks a month for over a year and a half.

"During those agonizing days, friends and church members tried their best to help the Bergrens. 'But most of my friends,' says Wendy, 'didn't know how to cope, or how to assist someone who was seriously ill with cancer.'

"In one of her darkest moments, she jotted down some ideas to share with her friends:

"1) Visit frequently but call before you come. Don't stay away so I can get my rest. Companionship is often more important than rest. She went on to say, 'I've discovered that loneliness is the greatest deterrent to sleep.'

"2) Ask me who I would like to see and invite them to come along. Sometimes I'm too tired to talk, but it's nice to listen.

"3) Take snapshots of my children over the months so I don't feel I've totally missed out on this part of their lives.

"4) Offer to run two small errands a week for the family.

"5) Allow me to feel sad and prepare for the worst.

"6) Tell me a joke. Even if it's not funny I'll laugh!

"7) Touch me. The isolation of being an invalid makes love's touch sweeter.

"8) Say the word cancer around me so I can feel normal.

"9) Tell me how good I look considering everything I've been through. (Someone told her she had to be the best looking bald woman in town and she loved it!)

"10) Offer to babysit — even if my husband and I stay home. This gives us the freedom of a private adult life in a place my illness can cope with.

"11) Encourage your husband to come over to visit my husband in the evenings. My illness has eliminated many of his pleasures. How happy I am when I hear him laughing with a friend in his shop or cheering Monday night football and popping popcorn with a pal!

"12) Pray for me and tell me that you're praying.

"13) Talk to me about the future. Planning for the future, birthdays, graduations, etc., increases my faith." (paraphrased)[1]

Janet Britton, author of *To Live Each Moment*, also had a malignant tumor and underwent a mastectomy followed by radiation and chemotherapy treatments lasting more than a year. During that entire time, her church family ministered to her and her family not only physically but also emotionally and spiritually. When it was all over, she said, "No one person or even ten people could have met all of our needs."[2]

She writes: "From the day of my hospital admittance my congregation banded together to care for our family's physical needs. They babysat our children while my husband visited me, canned green beans and tomatoes, and baked pies and cookies. Friends brought flowers, plants, cards and notes.

"At the hospital they washed and curled my hair, gave me manicures, and set guard duties so I could rest. One woman loaned me a shocking pink bed jacket to help me feel pretty, and another bought me herb teas and crackers to help me fight nausea. When I grew exhausted, they read my Bible to me and jotted my business and personal correspondence.

"After I was discharged, Genny, a registered nurse from our congregation, visited daily to change my dressings. The women's group organized evening meals for the week of my recovery. When I began radiation and chemotherapy treatments, dozens of church friends chauffeured me the 80-mile round trip to the hospital.

"Meals and baked goods poured in for months after formally organized meals had stopped. At Christmas, when fancy cookies are a must in the Britton home, church families contributed two dozen cookies each from their holiday baking and arranged a gigantic tray of delicacies.

"When spring-cleaning time arrived, little elves whisked through my house while I underwent treatment. Wallpaper I had bought for the kitchen miraculously appeared on the walls.

"The church also met our emotional needs. Friends encouraged my husband to talk openly about his fears of coping with long-term illness and possible death. Sensitive also to the children's fears, they took them to the Dairy Queen or to ball games.

"To lift my spirits, people popped in to take me out for lunch. The mailbox frequently contained thinking-of-you cards or notes of appreciation. Friends planned a surprise birthday party and gave me IOUs for dinner, gardening, window washing, etc.

"The greatest emotional gift, though, was touching — physically and emotionally. Friends sat beside me as I lay exhausted on our couch. They touched my shoulder, held my hand, kissed my cheek, hugged me; their touch cushioned me. They shared with me, as they always had, their marital problems, occupational problems, and personal difficulties. Their continued confidence reminded me that although physically impaired I was not mentally or emotionally damaged."[3]

Illness of any kind, especially a critical illness, produces stress. A compassionate and trained congregation can ease the physical strain and lighten the emotional load, as they did in Janet's case, but no one can eliminate it. No member of the family is immune, and research indicates that many marriages fail under the pressure. In addition to the obvious difficulties of maintaining anything resembling a normal home and lifestyle, there are also enormous psychological pressures — pressures which men and women react to in decidedly different ways, creating additional tension and misunderstanding.

The overriding feeling is often a sense of helplessness, especially when the critically ill patient is a child. Your child is suffering, perhaps even facing death, and there seems to be so little that you can do. Men, for the most part, respond to this sense of helplessness in two general ways — anger or escape, depending on their temperament.

An assertive man, who is used to taking charge and getting things done, will be tempted to anger by his inability to rectify the situation. He may take his feelings out on the doctors and other health professionals, accusing them of incompetence or worse; or, he may direct his anger toward members of his own family, especially his wife. His rage is really directed toward the disease which threatens his precious child, or toward God Who has "let" this happen, or even toward his own helplessness. But how do you direct your rage against something or someone you cannot get at? Hence his misdirected anger and the resulting emotional fallout.

Others simply "escape." They lose themselves in their work, or in taking care of the household chores and the other children. Frequently they deny the seriousness of the situation, refusing to face the possibility of their child's impending death. This effectively isolates them from both their spouse and their child. The resulting loneliness and resentment should be obvious.

Mothers, on the other hand, tend to invest themselves totally in the sick child at the expense of their husband and the other children. For them there is no world outside of that small hospital room, no concern except the welfare of their suffering child. When other concerns press upon them, they rationalize: Others will have to understand. This is an emergency, nothing else matters right now. The resulting jealousies and tensions only add to the family trauma.

And then there are the inevitable conflicts over marital intimacy. In times of sickness and death, men and women react to sex in remarkably different ways. Women tend to lose all interest, while men not infrequently exhibit, if not an increased desire, at least an ongoing interest.

While ministering to couples in the crisis of family illness, I have frequently heard wives complain about their husbands, "He's disgusting; how can he even think of sex at a time like this?" He, on the other hand, feels that his wife has an unhealthy fixation on the current crisis.

Repeatedly I've been able to help couples understand that each is coping with the crisis in the way most natural to them. The husband desires sexual intimacy with his wife as a way of shutting out the pain of present reality, at least for a few brief minutes. It's his way of affirming his faith in life and love even in the face of death itself. He desires such intimacy, not because he's an unfeeling brute, as she supposes, but because it's the only way he can cope with his pain and the impending loss.

Nor does his wife have an abnormal fixation on the sick child, as her husband accuses. She does not love her husband any less, she has not forgotten the other children, or the family's needs. It's just that right then her child is suffering, perhaps at the point of death, and all of her maternal instincts call her to rush to his defense. The fact that she can do nothing but maintain her bedside vigil does not, in any way, diminish her sense of responsibility. She does not explain her feelings, doesn't even imagine that she should. Doesn't he feel the same way? Isn't this his child too?

Once the couple has been helped to understand the legitimacy of each other's feelings, the validity of their individual responses, then they can move past resentments to acceptance, perhaps even to understanding. Such understanding enables them to face the common enemy (illness) united, arm in arm, rather than mistakenly attacking each other. Such mutual support is absolutely mandatory if they are to successfully negotiate this crisis.

In addition to explanation, perhaps even more than explanation, they need our presence and our emotional support as they face this critical illness.

Intuitively they realize that we are limited in what we can do. We cannot work miracles, though we can and should pray for one at the appropriate time. Nor can we answer the unanswerable "why" questions: Why is this happening to me? Why won't God heal our baby? Why. . .why. . .why? What we can and must do is be there. We must minister with our presence.

A few weeks ago a young couple in our congregation learned that the wife had a malignant tumor. It was, of course, disconcerting news, though the doctor's prognosis was as positive as one can be when a malignancy is involved. On the morning of the scheduled surgery, Brenda and I drove to the hospital, arriving just as the woman and her husband were getting out of their car. Consequently we were able to be with them as she was admitted to the hospital and prepared for surgery.

It was a tense time. Jerry, her husband, was quietly attentive to his young wife, not daring to miss a single moment of this precious time together. She was brave. Glad the waiting was almost over, eager to get the whole thing behind them.

Brenda and I listened as they made small talk about their boys, how just that morning the car had rolled out of the garage and was, this very minute, straddling the mailbox in front of their house, awaiting the arrival of the wrecker.

After a while the room grew still, each of us silently entertaining our own thoughts. Then I shared some scriptures and we all prayed. That's all, nothing more. Soon afterwards, the hospital attendants came for her and she was wheeled away into surgery.

Just yesterday we received a handwritten thank you note from her. To Brenda she wrote: "Thank you for loving, caring, crying, doing. . . . It meant so much to see you before my surgery. Richard is right when he says just being there is a blessing. Your presence, prayers, and concern made a difficult time bearable."

And to me she wrote: "Jerry and I were touched and loved when you and Brenda came to the hospital the morning of my surgery. I think it was neat of God to send you there early enough to escort us in from the parking lot. I just feel like we drew on your strength, just having you there. . . . Indirectly, we've also benefitted from your ministry. The way you've taught Christian Chapel to love and minister. No body of people could have loved us more."

Years ago, when I was just a kid preacher, I might have puzzled over her card, wondering how she could have possibly drawn strength from our presence, or comfort from the simple fact that we were there. Not any more though. I still don't understand how it works, but I know it does. Even when it seems we aren't doing much, when it seems that the best we can manage are silent tears, a quick hug, and a shared prayer, God makes it enough.

Sue Monk Kidd writes:

"Soon after midnight I rose from the tiny, sleepless cot in my husband's hospital room. He lay terribly sick. Beyond the window no moon shone. Not even a street lamp pierced the darkness that churned against the pane. It seemed the night conspired with the darkness in my soul. . .with the churning anguish I felt over my husband's precarious condition.

"As my fears blackened, I pulled on my shoes and fled out into the hospital corridor where dim artificial light laced the wall with shadows. Tears trembled on my face. . .a sob crowded my throat. A few feet away I saw the visitor's elevator, its door open. I ducked inside and fumbled with the buttons. As it swept me up, my sobs gave way, echoing anonymously along the elevator's silent pathway. I do not know how many times I rode up and down while my despair poured out. But it was the middle of the night, and who would notice?

"Suddenly I heard a soft ping. The elevator stopped. The doors opened. Inside stepped an elderly man with thinning white hair and eyes that searched the tears streaming down my face. He pushed a button, then dug into his pocket. As we lurched upward, he handed me a neatly folded handkerchief. I wiped my eyes, staring into his kind, steady gaze. And his compassion reached my heart like the first fingers of morning sun dispelling the night. God was strangely present in the little elevator, as if He were there in the old man's face.

"The doors swished open. I thanked the stranger and handed back his handkerchief, damp and soiled with my anguish. Then he nodded me a gentle smile and slipped away.

"As I returned to my husband's room, I was quite sure. . .God does not fail us in our distress. His compassion is everywhere. And the tenderest promise in the Bible is true — God shall wipe away every tear from their eyes.

"And He shall. . .one way or another."[4]

Now that's the tender touch, and that's "blue-collar Christianity" at its very best.

Footnotes:

1. Wendy Bergren, "Mom Is Very Sick — Here's How to Help" (Arcadia: Focus on the Family, 1982).

2. Janet Britton, *Well, Janet Told Me. . .* (*Moody Magazine,* Jan. 1985), p. 83.

3. Ibid, pp. 82, 83.

4. Sue Monk Kidd, quoted in *Dawnings, Finding God's Light in the Darkness,* edited by Phyllis Hobe (New York: Guideposts Associates, Inc., 1981), p. 88.

Chapter 6

THROUGH THE VALLEY

It was late Monday night,
or perhaps even early Tuesday morning,
about 1 a.m., I think.

As I was leaving St. John's Hospital,
I noticed three men huddled together
in the waiting room.

On the table between them I saw an open Bible.
Immediately I realized what was happening —
life was threatened,
a close friend or family member was in danger,
and the man of God was there,
bringing hope and encouragement.

The two younger men
listened intently as he spoke,
hanging on every word.
And not just the words either,
but his presence as well.

When accident or disease strikes,
when death threatens,
family members and friends want a word from God,
a healing word, an encouraging word, a word of hope.
Or better yet,
they want to experience the comfort of His presence,
they want to sense His nearness,
know that they are not alone.

And, as inconceivable as it may seem,
that is what we do,
every last one of us who call ourselves friends and
Christians.

We embody the presence of the Lord,
become His hand extended.
We listen with love,
absorb the hurt and fear without rebuke,
and when the time is right,
we speak words of hope and comfort!

As I watched from a distance,
I gained a new appreciation
for pastoral care,
for the ministry the Church is so often called to
provide.

Thanks, Lord,
for allowing us
to be Your personal representatives
in crucial times like these.
I, for one, am humbled and blessed.

Chapter 6

THROUGH THE VALLEY

Few things in life are more disconcerting than a diagnosis of terminal illness, whether it's your own or that of someone who is close to you. It came for John Claypool when the doctors told him that his eight-year-old daughter, Laura Lue, had acute leukemia. In *Tracks of a Fellow Struggler* he writes:

"She was a bright, exuberant child, full of life and joy. . .as she finished the second grade, and participated in two recitals in one day — a Suzuki violin performance on Saturday morning, and a ballet recital that evening.

"The next day she seemed tired, and we attributed it to her hyperactivity. But she stayed tired, and then her ankle began to swell and finally the pediatrician sent us to a specialist at Children's Hospital where on the third day we heard the words 'acute leukemia'.

"That was on Wednesday and I made no attempt to preach the following Sunday. . ."[1]

If you've never been there, if you've never heard the doctor say, "I'm sorry; it's malignant. . .inoperable. . .well, maybe some hope, but. . ." then you will probably have some difficulty fully appreciating the trauma Claypool experienced and that of others in similar circumstances. Watching someone you love die is a lonely experience, fully known only to those who have been there, and they seldom talk about it. Still, it's important for us to try to understand. How else can we minister comfort?

For the next eighteen months and ten days John and his family lived with death. There were months of desperate hope and terrible pain. A roller coaster ride of highs and lows. Periods of remission when hope was as exhilarating as the first barefoot day of spring, when death was nothing more than a distant shadow; followed by a major relapse when hope was shattered on the rocks of reality, when death returned, a taunting monster. Always it was there, even on the brightest days; and finally it won, or so it seemed.

"Just two weeks after Christmas, on a Saturday evening, with the snow falling softly outside the window, Laura Lue died in her own bed, in her own room."[2]

In times like that the Church rallies, rushing to do what she can for the bereaved. Soon the dining room table groans beneath the staggering assortment of food brought in by loving friends. No one really has much of an appetite at a time like that, but it's something we know how to do, it's something we can give. It's our unspoken way of saying that life goes on: Eat something, you'll feel better. Maybe not right away, but by-and-by, and you will see that the sun will shine again, that once more you will be able to laugh.

No one says any of this, at least not out loud. And they probably don't even think it, not consciously anyway. It's deeper than that, almost intuitive. We simply know that life goes on, that death will once again fade away. So we go on living, by rote, if necessary, until we find our way again.

Unfortunately, death doesn't fade very fast for those most affected by it. Long after the last casserole has been devoured, the serving dishes washed and returned; long after the last of the out-of-town relatives have said their goodbyes and made the long journey home; long after the most caring friends have gotten over their grief and returned to a normal life, the bereaved will still hurt. Death's residue will hang on like a stubborn toothache.

And then, more than ever, they will need the ministry of comfort. Not covered dishes and sympathy cards, but a safe place where they can grieve without being rebuked or even misunderstood. They also need a safe person, someone who will let them be real, someone who will let them weep or rage, as the case may be. Someone who won't try to explain the unexplainable, or fix everything with a prayer. What they will need, then, is a good listener — and lots of Kleenex.

In the case of terminal illness, the actual ministry of comfort starts earlier, much earlier, before death, with the doctor's diagnosis, as soon as the patient and his family learn that according to medical science there is no hope. Studies conducted by Dr. Elizabeth Kubler-Ross, best known for her works on death and dying, indicate that most patients facing death experience five emotional stages.

The first stage is denial: "It can't be. They must be wrong. Someone in the lab made a mistake." During the denial stage, many patients go from doctor to doctor seeking a favorable diagnosis.

The second stage is anger: "Why, God, why? Why me? Why not someone else? It's not fair. Why should I be smitten in the prime of life and some deviant enjoy perfect health?"

The third stage is bargaining: "God if You will help me, I will live the rest of my life for You. I will give 20 percent of my income to the Church. If You will let me live to see my son graduate from high school, or my daughter get married, or the birth of my first grandchild, then I'll die without a fuss..."

Stage four is depression. Nothing has worked. Not denial, not anger and not bargaining. Illness is real, pain is real, death looms ever larger. During this stage patients often become non-communicative. They turn their faces to the wall and wish to die, wish to get it over with. Frequently they resist all medical treatment and, in short, give up.

The fifth stage is acceptance. Acceptance, not resignation. To be resigned is to give up, to lose all hope, to say that whatever will be will be. Acceptance, on the other hand, acknowledges the reality of the situation without losing hope. The patient realizes that death is inevitable unless there's a medical breakthrough or a divine intervention, but he does not give up. Nor does he waste what precious time he has left in either anger or denial. During this stage he begins preparing for the end, getting his affairs in order and bidding his goodbyes.

During this time, before death, the patient's family is both care-giver and bereaved. They are care-givers in the sense that they are the first line of spiritual and emotional support for the patient. Yet in another sense, by virtue of their intimate relationship with the dying person, they are in need of ministry themselves. Theirs is an almost impossible task. They are not only expected to be emotionally and physically present for the terminally ill family member, but they must maintain the family's daily life as well. Not infrequently the burden is more than they can bear, at least more than they can bear alone.

This is where the ministry of comfort comes in, but comfort doesn't come easy to very many. Most of us have never walked this way before. We do not know what the dying person or his family really feels, wants or expects of us. As a result, we tend to avoid the dying and the bereaved. Even when we do discipline ourselves to "do our duty" (that is, even if we don't avoid them physically), we often isolate the bereaved emotionally by avoiding any reference to their illness or possible death.

H. Norman Wright identifies this whole process as the *abandonment syndrome*. He lists four stages: 1) a brief formal monologue; 2) the nonperson reaction; 3) ignoring or rejecting the cues that the person attempts to give; and 4) literal abandonment.[3]

During the first of these stages, people (even doctors and nurses) breeze in and out, communicating only on a superficial level. They usually ask a few rhetorical questions, then leave without letting the person express his inner feelings. As Christians, we often resort to prayer in these times, especially when the feeling being expressed becomes too painful for us.

One lady, a victim of cancer, told me that her pastor would breeze in and out of her room, chatting all the time, hardly giving her a chance to get a word in edgeways. He did ask how she was doing, but not in a way that encouraged her to respond honestly. After a bit, he would pray, and then he was gone.

Well, after awhile she had had all she could take and she determined that he was going to hear her out. When he arrived for his next visit, she was ready. He breezed in with his usual chatter and superficial questions: "How are you feeling today? Did you sleep well? Are you having much pain?" Then she unloaded on him. Not in anger, just honestly. She told him that the pain was absolutely intolerable; that she was afraid of dying; that she prayed day and night but it seemed that God was gone, that He never answered her, never made His presence known. By this time the pastor was obviously uncomfortable, and when she paused for a breath he said, "Let's pray."

Always before she had meekly followed his lead, but not today.

"Don't do that to me," she said. "You're always using prayer like some kind of escape hatch. Every time I start to tell you what it's really like to be barely thirty, the mother of two, and dying with cancer, you want to pray. That's not real prayer. It's just religious words, a smoke screen, so you can make your escape. Today you are going to hear me out; you're going to walk with me through this valley of the shadow of death. That's what you're supposed to do, you know. That's why you're here — so I don't have to face death alone."

He stayed until she finished, let's give him that, but it was a long time before he visited her again.

I share that incident not to discredit the man, or the ministry, but as a way of graphically illustrating a common tactic we Christians use, unconsciously I'm sure, to escape the terrible pain that is so much a part of terminal illness. It's not that we consciously misuse prayer, but when faced with impossible situations, we gravitate to it naturally, almost by second nature. Most of the time that's as it should be, but in this case it effectively isolates the dying person, and prayer was never meant to do that.

Timing and sensitivity are the keys here. Or as one grieving father said, following his son's untimely death, "I know all the 'right Biblical passages'. . . But the point is this: While the words of the Bible are true, grief renders them unreal."

The same thing can be said about prayer. There is nothing, absolutely nothing, more powerful than prayer; yet suffering and grief can render it unreal too. That is not to say that there will never be a time for prayer in the sickroom, but only that the time will seldom come before we have listened deeply and with compassion to the honest concerns of the dying and their family members.

Such a ministry is not without great cost. There's something painfully disturbing about watching a person die, whether it takes a few hours or several weeks. Death seems to mock us, to render our best efforts, our latest medical technology, even our most earnest prayers, impotent. It brings us face to face with our own mortality, a subject we've mostly been able to dismiss in the rush of living. But here in the sick room, it catches us by the throat, looks us in the eye, demands our full attention.

John Claypool, describing his own journey through the valley of the shadow of death as he watched his eight-year-old daughter battle acute leukemia, writes:

"I perhaps need to confess to you that at times in the past few months I have been tempted to conclude that our whole existence is utterly absurd. More than once I looked radical doubt full in the face and honestly wondered if all our talk about love and purpose and a fatherly God were not simply a veil of fantasy that we pathetic humans had projected against the void.....There were the times, for example, when Laura Lue was hurting so intensely that she had to bite on a rag and used to beg me to pray to God to take away that awful pain. I would kneel down beside her bed and pray with all the faith and conviction of my soul, and nothing would happen except the pain continuing to rage on. Or again, that same negative conclusion tempted when she asked me in the dark of the night: 'When will this leukemia go away?' I answered: 'I don't know, darling, but we are doing everything we know to make that happen.' Then she said: 'Have you asked God when it will go away?' And I said: 'Yes, you have heard me pray to him many times.' But she persisted: 'What did He say? When did He say it would go away?' And I had to admit to myself he had not said a word! I had done a lot of talking and praying and pleading, but the reponse of the heavens had been silence."[4]

This, I believe, is what Jesus was talking about when He asked James and John, ". . .'Can you drink the cup I drink or be baptized with the baptism I am baptized with?' " (Mark 10:38). Not, can you drink your own cup of death; not, can you remain faithful unto death; not, can you die your own martyr's death; but, can you walk with Me through My suffering and death? Do you have the stomach for it? Can you minister comfort to Me when you know you can't really change anything; when all you can do is be there while I die, so I don't have to face those last hours alone?

Will you be able to bear it when the Romans get done with their thorns and their whips; when My face is chalky white from loss of blood; when My back is raw ribbons of mutilated flesh; when I stagger, weak from more pain than I could have ever imagined it possible for a man to bear? Or will you turn away, unable to bear it? When you see Me writhing in excruciating pain, and you can't so much as cool My fevered flesh; when you hear My strangled cry of thirst; when you sense the darkness and aloneness that surrounds both inside and out; when you hear My soul's anguished cry, "My God, My God, why have You forsaken Me?" will you comfort Me then?

John was there to the bitter end, as was Mary, the mother of Jesus, and Mary Magdalene and several others. Peter too, but at the far edge of the crowd, as far away as possible. Did they drink that cup as they so confidently said they could? Hardly. They sipped it maybe, choking on its painful dregs, gagging, so bitter was it, but they couldn't drink it.

It's interesting, isn't it, that the women outnumbered the men several times over. Not, I think, because women are braver than men, but because comfort comes more natural for them. The women in Jesus' life understood that He would draw strength just from the sight of them, that their presence would be a comfort to Him. Besides, they wanted to be there; they couldn't imagine letting Him die alone.

The ministry of comfort, on the other hand, is especially hard for men, for those of us who are used to getting things done. It's hard on us to sit and wait — to watch, powerless, as death claims its prey. We want to do something, anything. We must exert our authority, regain control of our world. But what can we do in such seemingly impossible cases? Pray maybe? Or pretend the one we love isn't hurting and dying?

Our need to do something, anything, is almost unbearable. Taking action gives us a feeling of being in control again. We're not, of course, but it seems we are — and that makes us feel better. Yet when we allow our discomfort to inititate action, we usually do the wrong thing.

For instance, when Jesus tried to tell the disciples of His impending suffering and death in Jerusalem at the hands of the chief priests, "Peter took him aside and began to rebuke him. 'Never Lord!' he said. 'This shall never happen to you!' " (Matt. 16:22).

How like stage three in H. Norman Wright's abandonment syndrome when family and friends ignore or reject the cues that the dying person attempts to give. For instance, patients often say things like, "I don't have much to look forward to any more," or perhaps something even more direct, "I think I am going to die soon." Unfortunately, many people respond by changing the subject or with such nonsense as: "Don't talk like that. You're going to live for years. Why, you'll probably outlive me." While the conscious intent may be to bring cheer, it seldom, if ever, works. Instead, such a response effectively isolates the patient, leaving him to face death alone.

The underlying motive, unconscious for the most part, is to escape our own pain which is brought on by the patient's candid discussion of his true feelings. We are not yet ready to honestly acknowledge either his impending death or our personal loss.

This situation usually leads to the fourth stage, which is literal abandonment. When a person is ill, with a nonfatal disease, the nurse may have to hang a sign on his door restricting visitors. When the diagnosis is "terminal," people begin withdrawing voluntarily. It has also been observed that some loved ones initially have close contact with the terminally ill person, such as kissing him on the lips. Then they begin to kiss him only on the forehead, then the hand, and finally they simply blow a kiss from across the room. Tragically, the patient gets the message.

Go with me to Gethsemane, on the night of our Lord's betrayal. The scriptures record it this way: ". . .he (Jesus) began to be deeply distressed and troubled" (Mark 14:33). Hear Him as He speaks to Peter, James and John: " 'My soul is overwhelmed with sorrow to the point of death,' he said to them. 'Stay here and keep watch' " (v. 34). Which is to say: Don't leave Me alone with this. Stay with Me through these awful hours. I need you now as I have never needed you before.

"Can you drink the cup I am going to drink?" He had asked them some days earlier.

"We can," they assured Him, but can they?

This is the moment of truth, and they can't drink it. The cup is too bitter, the pain too real. They can't even bear to look. They abandon Him — not literally, that comes later. Now they simply escape into the sweet oblivion of sleep. Three times He attempts to arouse them, three times He appeals to them for their support, but still they turn from the cup of His sufferings.

Mark says, ". . .They did not know what to say to him" (Mark 14:40). How like most of us they were; or more likely, how like them we are. Wordless before such sorrow, tongue-tied and fumbling, never realizing that our presence is all He wants. Not words, not theological explanations, just our presence.

So it is ultimately for all who look death in the eye, whether they be a terminally ill patient slowly dying, or the grieving loved one. When we reduce it to the lowest common denominator, what they want from us, what they expect from us, is nothing more or less than our presence.

Some years ago, when I was pastoring The Church of the Comforter in Craig, Colorado, I answered a frantic pounding on my door and found myself face to face with a grief-stricken man. Between sobs he told me that his seventeen-year-old son had been killed when a tractor rolled over on him. Shattered though he was, he was not seeking my help for himself, but for his wife who was outside in the car, beside herself, hysterical.

When I got to the car, she was rocking back and forth, crying from the deepest part of her being — great gasping sobs. As I slid into the seat beside her, I heard her praying, asking the Lord to raise her son from the dead.

What did I do? Nothing. Well, almost nothing. Without a word I put my arm around her shoulders and took one of her tightly clenched fists in my hand. For several minutes more she continued her violent sobbing and her desperate prayer. Finally she began to succumb to exhaustion and, little by little, she grew quiet. What did I say then? Very little. I mean, what is there to say at a time like that? I just held her and wept silently, allowing the Holy Spirit to minister comfort through the gift of my presence.

The ministry of comfort is really very simple — not easy, but simple. The most important thing is presence; be there, don't desert. We are usually pretty good about being there in the moment of crisis, but as the days grow into weeks, we have a tendency to get so caught up in life that we have less and less time for the bereaved.

Remember, grieving is a slow process, often requiring two years or more to complete its healing work, and it can't be hurried. Certain times will be more difficult than others — holidays, anniversaries, birthdays and, of course, the anniversary of the death. We must never make a special point of reminding grieving people of their loss, or of pointing out the significance of any given day. But we should be conscious of them and make a special effort to be available during those difficult times.

In addition to our early absence, we are often fumbling in our efforts to comfort. I'm not talking about the tongue-tied mourner who comes and holds the hand of the bereaved person because he can't think of anything to say, so great is his sense of loss. That sensitive soul inadvertently provides more comfort than a dozen scripture-quoting comforters.

Don't misunderstand me. I'm not making light of the eternal scriptures. I'm just pointing out that there is a time to speak, and a time to be silent. There is a time for quoting scripture, a time when the great passages will comfort and sustain as nothing else will, but that time is seldom during the early stages of grief. That's a time to just be there, a time for an arm around the shoulder, a supporting hand.

So often we try to fix things, we try to say something that will make the pain go away. Usually when we do, we only make things worse.

For instance, a few days after I had preached the funeral for that seventeen-year-old boy, I went to visit the grieving parents and found them, especially the mother, wrestling with lots of guilt. Now that's not unusual in the days immediately following the death of a loved one. All of us, I'm sure, can think of things we wish we had done differently, things we wish we had or had not said. But this was different, and I sensed that almost immediately.

A well-meaning, but insensitive and ill-advised friend had scolded the mother for crying. "Your son was a Christian, wasn't he?" she had reasoned. "Well then, he's in heaven with the Lord, so dry your tears and rejoice."

How do you suppose that had made the grieving mother feel? Guilty and confused, I can tell you. No doubt she felt that if she really believed, then maybe she wouldn't be crying; yet she hurt so bad, her loss was so great, her wound so raw, she couldn't stop. And if she hurt this badly, did that mean she wasn't a true believer?

Of course not. Her grief had very little to say about the quality of her faith, but a whole lot to say about how much she loved her son. Then again maybe it did have something to say about her faith. It takes great faith, does it not, to trust God with your anger and your pain, to let Him know how you really feel on the inside, behind the brave face you put on for your Christian friends, beneath the calm exterior you present to the world?

How, you may be wondering, should we respond then to someone who is expressing a lot of hurt and anger? Let Jesus be our model.

Following the death of Lazarus, Jesus went to minister to the family, especially Martha and Mary. When Martha heard He was coming, she rushed to meet Him and immediately began pouring out her heart. " 'Lord,' Martha said to Jesus, 'if You had been here, my brother would not have died' " (John 11:21).

Her first response is anger. She accuses Jesus of failing, of not caring, of ignoring them in their hour of greatest need. What does Jesus do? How does He respond? He absorbs her anger without rebuke. He understands how things must seem from her limited perspective, how much she loved her brother and how deeply she hurts.

Yet Martha doesn't stop there. Even in her anger, her faith expresses itself: ". . .'I know he will rise again in the resurrection at the last day. . . . I believe that you are the Christ, the Son of God, who was to come into the world' " (John 11:24,27).

When she quickly moves from anger to faith, Jesus meets her there and builds on her confession. He says to her, ". . .'I am the resurrection and the life. He who believes in me will live, even though he dies; and whoever lives and believes in me will never die. Do you believe this?' " (John 11:25). And Martha cries, " 'Yes, Lord. . . .' " (v. 27).

Mary responds differently. She too is hurt and angry, maybe more hurt than angry in keeping with her temperament.

"When Mary reached the place where Jesus was and saw him, she fell at his feet and said, 'Lord, if you had been here, my brother would not have died.'

"When Jesus saw her weeping. . ., he was deeply moved in spirit and troubled. . . .[and] Jesus wept" (John 11:32,33,35).

Notice that Jesus also meets Mary where she is. And there's little or no faith in her confession, beyond the faith to tell Jesus how she really feels. Somehow, even in her grief and disappointment, she believes He will understand, and He does. For her, He has no theological pronouncements, no revelation about resurrection life, no discourses about His divine sonship. Why? Not because they are any less true now, but because she is not ready to receive them. There's nothing in her heart but sorrow and tears, so He meets her there. He weeps with her.

What am I trying to say? Simply this: when ministering to the grieving, meet them where they are. If they are expressing honest faith, reflect honest faith back to them. If they are raging, pouring out their hurt and anger, absorb that without rebuke. Don't censure them. And don't try to explain why this terrible tragedy has happened to them. Listen with love. Weep with them. Remember, it is all right to say you don't know. Life is filled with mystery, and faith doesn't mean we have all the answers as much as it means we trust God unconditionally even when there seem to be no answers.

Some of the most faulty theology I've ever heard has been the product of a misguided attempt to explain an unexplainable sickness or death. I've heard people say, "God must have His reason," as if there were something magical about suffering and death, something only God understands.

I'll grant you there are people who have turned their sufferings and tragedies into testimonies. But more often than not, the opposite is true. People have cracked under the strain, marriages have broken up after the death of a child, survivors have grown cynical and bitter.

I don't understand why suffering and death strike one and not another, but I reject unequivocally the assumption that God is the cause or that tragedy is His will. Maybe He allows these terrible things; for certain He stands ready to help us cope with our tragedies, to walk with us through the valley of the shadow of death.

Harold Kushner speaks to these issues in his book, *When Bad Things Happen to Good People.* He writes: "I was once called on to help a family through an almost unbearable tragedy. This middle-aged couple had one daughter, a bright nineteen-year-old college freshman. One morning they received a phone call from the university infirmary: 'We have bad news. Your daughter collapsed while walking to class. A blood vessel burst in her brain, and she died before we could do anything. We're terribly sorry. . . .' I went over to see them that same day. I expected anger, shock, grief; but I didn't anticipate their first words, 'You know, Rabbi, we didn't fast Yom Kippur.' " (paraphrased)[5]

"Why did they think they were somehow responsible for this tragedy? Who taught them to believe in a God who would strike down a gifted young woman as punishment for some one else's ritual infraction?"[6]

Jesus too rejected that kind of simplistic, cause-and-effect reasoning when He was asked about the Galileans whom Pilate had killed.

" 'Do you think,' He asked, 'that these Galileans were worse sinners than all other Galileans because they suffered this way? I tell you, no!....Or those eighteen who died when the tower in Siloam fell on them — do you think they were more guilty than all the others living in Jerusalem? I tell you, no!....' " (Luke 13:2-5).

Jesus did not explain either of those tragedies, but He did make it emphatically clear that neither the victims nor their families were to blame for what happened to them.

I tend to be pretty hard on myself when I can't adequately explain suffering or death, but maybe in light of Jesus' example I should be content with explaining what it is not. Or better yet, maybe we should content ourselves with ministering comfort to the bereaved.

Some months ago, I received a phone call from a man who had visited our church a time or two. He was obviously hurting. The doctors had just informed him that his father had cancer throughout his body and they gave him only a few months to live. I listened quietly while he poured his heart out, occasionally reflecting his statements back to him. But I made no attempt to explain the mystery of why this was happening to his father. Nor did I attempt to encourage him with false assurances. After about twenty-five minutes, he grew quiet and I shared a passage of scripture and we prayed. As he was preparing to end our conversation, he kept telling me how much I had helped, kept thanking me for encouraging him. Really I had done nothing more than listen with genuine concern. I had not said more than a half-dozen sentences, and yet he was comforted.

Once more I learned that the key to ministering to the bereaved is gentleness and compassion, just being there. Or as Joe Bayley says, "Don't try to prove anything to a survivor. An arm around the shoulder, a firm grip of the hand, a kiss — these are the proofs grief needs, not logical reasoning."

Footnotes

1. John Claypool, *Tracks of a Fellow Struggler* (Waco: Word Publishers, Inc., 1974), p. 21.

2. Ibid., p. 65.

3. H. Norman Wright, *Training Christians to Counsel* (Denver: Christian Marriage Enrichment), p. 136.

4. Claypool, p. 77.

5. Harold S. Kushner, *When Bad Things Happen to Good People* (New York: Avon Books, 1981), p. 8.

6. Ibid., p. 8.

Chapter 7

UNUSUAL PEACE

She was beside herself.
Internal storms of doubt and fear
lashed at her troubled soul.
She was like an exposed nerve,
raw and screaming.

Her husband had a history of unfaithfulness,
and now it was well past midnight,
and he still wasn't home.

Her imagination,
conditioned by past experience, created a series of
tormenting scenes.

Was he with another woman? Unfaithful again?
Was he, even now, writhing in excruciating pain,
the victim of a tragic auto accident?
Was he lying somewhere in a diabetic coma?

Once again her agitated emotions gave birth
to a series of unholy thoughts.
Anger swept over her,
leaving her hot and flushed,
cruelly vindictive and ready for revenge.

Then came fear,
like an icy hand on her heart,
cold and paralyzing.
Followed, almost without interruption,
by feelings of rejection and failure.

She wasn't good enough,
    pretty enough,
        smart enough.
Jealousy stood in the shadows of her mind,
    taunting her, manipulating her imagination,
        playing her like a puppet on a string.

Gently I took her hands in mine,
and when I did,
I had a vision of Jesus,
standing in the prow of a tiny ship.
He stood there, majestically,
while the winds lashed at Him
and the angry waves drenched Him
with salt spray.

Then He spoke a single word: "Peace!"
Instantly the sea was calm,
the wind hardly more than breath.

"Jesus," I prayed,
"Speak peace to her troubled soul.
Calm the raging storms of doubt and fear."
And, like a miracle, she grew quiet.
Peace reigned,
where only moments before chaos had been king.
Nothing had really changed, yet everything was
different!

Her husband still wasn't home,
and he hadn't called,
yet her fear and anger were gone,
at least for the moment.

I excused myself
and drove home through the still night,
marveling again at the peace of God which passes all
understanding.

Chapter 7

UNUSUAL PEACE

Before you read any further, take a moment and create in your mind a scene depicting peace. Imagine the circumstances, the environment, the situation which would enable you to be totally at peace.

Complete the picture. Fill in the colors and sounds, the details.

Go ahead. Put your finger between the pages of this book, close it, and don't open it again until you have the completed scene firmly fixed in your mind.

Did you imagine a tranquil scene? Perhaps a young mother in a moment of blissful rest, gently rocking her sleeping baby. A relaxing stroll through the park at the end of a demanding day. A good book in front of a warm fire on a winter evening. A second cup of coffee after you've got your husband off to work and the children safely on the school bus. A beautiful sunset. A child snugly tucked in bed, quiet in sleep, looking almost cherubic in the soft glow of the night light.

That's peace, all right, and it's wonderful, but it's not necessarily the peace of God — at least not a full revelation of it.

That kind of peace is conditional, dependent on outward circumstances. The peace of God, on the other hand, is not dependent on anything but God Himself, and it transcends all understanding. It's peace of a most unusual kind.

I should know, I've had several experiences in which His supernatural peace simply possessed me. None, however, more vivid than the time we thought our daughter Leah was dying.

It started with a low-grade fever, followed by vomiting which lasted for a couple of days. Since she was only eight months old and appeared to be dehydrating, we decided to take her to a pediatrician. After examining her, the doctor gave her an injection. When he did, she suffered a severe seizure.

Quickly the doctor ordered a second injection, and when that failed to control the convulsions, he ordered a third which also proved futile. By now Brenda and I were almost beside ourselves. Any illusions we had about the seriousness of the situation were shattered when the doctor scooped Leah's rigid body into his arms and ran for his car. Brenda and his nurse followed and in seconds they were racing for the hospital.

I rushed after them in my own car, fear pushing me ever closer to the point of panic. It seemed that all I could see was Leah's tiny body, rigid and spastic, her eyes rolled back in her head. Would I ever see her smile again, hear her giggle contentedly as Brenda pinned a dry diaper on her freshly powdered bottom?

Terrifying thoughts of death, Leah's death, our baby's death, tried to take control of my mind. With a Herculean effort I dismissed them, only to have them return a minute later and with a vengeance. There were other thoughts too, almost as terrifying — Leah, brain-damaged or growing up afflicted with epilepsy.

I skidded to a stop in the hospital parking lot just in time to see the doctor rush Leah into a specially equipped emergency area. For the next two and one-half hours the doctors worked to save her life. Brenda and I were left alone to await the outcome. In desperation I called my family and Brenda's, begging them to pray. Distinctly I can recall the desolation that washed over me after I hung up. Standing beside the now silent phone, at the end of the empty hallway, I felt totally alone.

After getting hold of myself, I made my way back to where Brenda was nervously pacing the floor just outside the emergency area. We clung to each other and cried and prayed. Together we faced the harsh reality — Leah might not live, and if she did, she might never be the same again. Never had life seemed so empty of hope, so crowded with pain and fear. Yet even as we came to grips with the terrifying possibility of Leah's death and all that would mean to us, we also began to sense God's presence and His peace.

The possibility of Leah's death was not diminished, it was no less real. Yet in a way that defies imagination, we were suddenly at peace. Until that moment, I had wondered how anyone survived the death of a child. Now I understood — at least in part, at least as much as anyone who hasn't lost a child can understand. This was what we used to sing about: ". . . He giveth more grace as the burdens grow greater. . ."[1] Somehow we were possessed of the assurance that no matter what happened, whether Leah lived or died, God's grace would be sufficient. Somehow life would still be worth living.

Finally the doctor emerged, looking exhausted but relieved. Leah was out of danger, she would live. The medical staff wanted to keep her in the hospital for a few more days. There were a number of tests they wanted to run. The doctor listened patiently as we bombarded him with a host of questions and concerns. After answering as best he could, he excused himself and we were left alone once again.

Only we weren't alone — God was with us! We were relieved, yet not nearly to the extent I had expected. The real relief had already come — the peace of God that passes all understanding.

About then Leah was wheeled out of the emergency area and Brenda gasped. She was clothed only in a diaper, her hands and feet were fastened to the rungs of the crib with cloth cords, and an IV was flowing into a vein in her head. We followed as she was taken into the nursery. For a long time we simply stood beside her tiny bed watching her sleep, relieved somehow just by the gentle motion of her breathing. The storm wasn't over but the crisis had passed, at least for the moment, and I found myself examining the peace that possessed me.

A story came to mind. Something I had read somewhere, or maybe heard in a sermon. It was about a group of artists who were asked to paint pictures depicting peace. Most of them produced paintings of the kinds of things you would expect — a quiet meadow at sunset, a mother and child, an empty sanctuary bathed in the refracted light of stained glass.

One picture, however, was different, totally different. It was a violent scene. The sky was stormy black, rent by jagged flashes of lightning. A lone tree, stubbornly clinging to a rocky cliff, was bent before the fierce wind, and angry breakers crashed on the jutting rocks at the base of the cliff where it met the sea.

"How," someone asked, "can such a violent storm depict peace?"

The artist was standing nearby and overheard the question. Joining the group of onlookers, he encouraged them to re-examine the picture, to notice not only the obvious but the detail as well.

Suddenly someone exclaimed, "I see it! I see it!" Pointing, he said, "Look, there in the cleft of the rock. There's a bird singing."

When I first heard that story, it was a good illustration. Now it was a profound truth, a truth I had experienced for myself. I was that tiny bird, sheltered in the cleft of the rock. All around me a storm was raging. Sickness and death threatened my only child, yet I had peace. Now the storm was easing a little and I took comfort in that. Still the true source of my confidence came from a sense of God's presence and the peace it brought.

Such peace is not unique to me. The annals of Christianity are filled with such experiences. Take the story of Elaine St. Johns, for instance. She experienced God's supernatural peace following a serious automobile accident. She writes:

"It does not take long for a car to go over a cliff. One instant the convertible in which I was a passenger was right side up on the night-black, mountainous Topanga Canyon Road between the bright lights of the San Fernando Valley and the beach houses on the Pacific Ocean. The next instant it was upside down in a tangle of scrub and brush far below. And I was pinned under the car fully conscious, paralyzed from the neck down.

"It should have been one of the darkest moments of my life.

"But it wasn't.

"For between that one instant and the next, I had actually felt God's presence. It came as an inner voice repeating three times the beautiful promise, 'Lo, I am with you alway' (Matthew 28:20). Simultaneously I entered into a timeless moment where the love of God was a substance — comforting, warm, light-bright, peace-filled, enveloping.

"The moment passed, but the peace, His peace, remained.

"Subsequent events unfolded rapidly. I smelled gas fumes. I called to my driver-companion — he had been thrown clear and was confused, but unhurt — to turn off the ignition. All at once, although I had no medical competence, I knew my neck was 'broken.' I asked my companion to pull me out from under the wreckage firmly, steadily, holding both feet. As he did so, the spinal cord was released from pressure. Feeling returned. (Later we were told how dangerous this procedure was, to be attempted only in surgery after a series of x-rays, and then not always successful.)

"A car came along the lonely road, stopped, two men carried me carefully up the cliff, drove me to a hospital, and disappeared. (Again, a most dangerous procedure, yet it could have been hours before we were discovered, and, since we were in a no-man's land which was in controversy between ambulances from the Valley and the coast — more hours before help arrived.)

"At the hospital the doctors waited for me to go into shock. I never did. Nor did I lose my calm during the medical crises and emergencies of the ensuing weeks.

"All this, the hospital staff decided, was a series of minor miracles. I knew it wasn't. It was the result of one great miracle, that moment in which I experienced God's love.

"I had labored long, sometimes very discouraged, in an effort to receive Christ's work 'in an honest and good heart, and bring forth fruit with patience' (Luke 8:15). Too often it seemed that patience itself was to be the chief fruitage. Then in a moment of extremity, when I could do nothing of myself, when I had no time to labor, or pray, or even think, the fruitage appeared as instant grace — 'Lo, I am with you always.'

"And He was."[2]

In one sense, the peace of God that Elaine St. Johns experienced was the result of His sovereign grace. Suddenly, instantly, she possessed it — or more likely, it possessed her. She didn't do anything to generate it. It was just there!

Yet in a deeper and more profound sense, it was the consequence of her spiritual disciplines. For some time she had been preparing for this moment, or one like it. Daily she had been hiding the Word in her heart, had been tuning her ear for God's voice. "Then," to use her words, "in a moment of extremity, when I could do nothing of myself, when I had no time to labor, or pray, or even think, the fruitage appeared as instant grace — 'Lo, I am with you always.' "[3]

You may be struggling with an overwhelming situation right now, or perhaps you know and love someone who is. Yet you don't have the peace of God, fear and anxiety have invaded your life, leaving you tormented and alone. What, you may be wondering, can you to do to find His peace?

First, change your focus. When you are in the midst of a difficult situation, it is easy to become preoccupied with your adversities, to become problem-centered, as it were, rather than God-centered. The problem-centered person seems to be looking at God through the wrong end of a telescope — He looks small and far away — as a result, his life is dominated by seemingly insurmountable problems and he is driven to despair.

The God-centered person, on the other hand, focuses on God's sufficiency, on His love and His presence, and like the Apostle Paul concludes, "...If God is for us, who can be against us?" (Rom. 8:31). He does not deny the reality of his problems, but he does put them into perspective.

Let me give you an example of how I overcome my fears, or at least how I manage them. I call it "worse case scenario." Here's how it works:

Let's return to the afternoon when Leah suddenly suffered life-threatening convulsions. Once I accepted the seriousness of the situation, I began to play it out in my mind. I considered all of the possibilities and played each one out to the bitter end, including the possibility of her death. At each step, I asked myself if God's grace was sufficient to cope with that possibility. The ultimate answer, of course, concerned death. If Leah died, would God's grace be enough?

Pacing that hospital hallway, I wrestled with that question. My fear wasn't for Leah. If she died, she would be with Jesus, free from all suffering and pain, never to know the sorrow or disappointment that is so much a part of this life. No, my concern was for Brenda and for me.

Death, as author Joe Baylay so aptly put it, is a wound to the living, and I wanted to know if we could survive. Other parents who had lost children came to mind, some I knew personally and some I had only read about. I remembered their pain, but I also remembered their hope, and I was encouraged. Finally, I concluded that God's grace was greater even than death, and I found myself quoting Romans 8:35,37-39:

"Who shall separate us from the love of Christ? Shall trouble or hardship or persecution or famine or nakedness or danger or sword?. . .No, in all these things we are more than conquerors through him who loved us. For I am convinced that neither death nor life, neither angels nor demons, neither the present nor the future, nor any powers, neither height nor depth, nor anything else in all creation, will be able to separate us from the love of God that is in Christ Jesus our Lord."

As I've already told you, the peace of God enveloped Brenda and me even before we knew Leah was out of danger. Some of that was simply a manifestation of His sovereign grace. But on another level, it was the result of our mindset, our confidence in His sufficiency. We knew that God was able to heal our little girl and we also knew that if she wasn't healed, He was able to mend our broken hearts and infuse our shattered lives with renewed joy and purpose. By reminding ourselves continually of those truths, we found His peace in the midst of a life-threatening crisis.

Most people, I'm convinced, can overcome almost any hardship if they are assured of three things. First, they must know that God cares. Then they must be certain that God is with them, that He won't abandon them, that He won't leave them alone with their pain. And finally, they have to have the assurance that He will redeem their situation; that is, that He will make it contribute in some way to their ultimate Christlikeness.

As rational creatures, the thought that a tragic accident or illness might be pointless, wasted, is simply unbearable to us. If we can be convinced that God will ultimately bring good out of what looks for all the world like a senseless tragedy, we can somehow bear it.

Do you remember the time Jesus and His disciples got caught at sea in a terrible storm? Mark records it: "A furious squall came up, and the waves broke over the boat, so that it was nearly swamped. Jesus was in the stern, sleeping on a cushion. The disciples woke him and said to him, 'Teacher, don't you care if we drown?' " (Mark 4:37,38). Like many of us when we are caught in a personal crisis, they wondered if Jesus was concerned about what was happening to them. They cried, " '...don't you *care* if we drown?' "

I'm thinking of a young couple from our church who spent two years on the mission field. While there, their second child was stillborn. It was a devastating blow. Here they were, thousands of miles from family and friends, laying their lives on the line for the sake of the kingdom, doing exactly what God had called them to do, so why did their baby die? How many times, I wonder, did they cry, "Lord, don't You care?"

A grieving mother comes to mind. Much of her life has been fraught with hardship. She married a soldier who brought her to the United States following his tour of duty. Shortly after the birth of their first child, he left her for another woman. Alone in a strange country, with a baby to care for, she must have wondered, "Lord, don't You care?"

Her child, she soon discovered, was severely epileptic, requiring constant medication and care, plus special schooling. "Lord, don't You care?"

Finally, at the age of sixteen, the young man was enrolled in public school and it seemed that, at last, he was entering the mainstream of life. Then in a freak accident, he drowned. Somehow he was left alone in the swimming pool following P.E. class, and apparently he suffered a seizure. Again the mother cried, "Lord, don't You care?"

Those are extreme cases, I'll grant you, but they are not nearly as isolated as I once thought. After more than twenty years in the pastorate, I'm realizing more and more just how many people live with pain, how many people suffer in silence and hide their sorrow behind a public smile. Over and over they have pled with me for an answer. "Doesn't God care?" they ask, or, "Why doesn't God *do* something?"

It's not really answers they want, but assurance. Intuitively, they realize that the "why" questions are beyond us.

Sometimes I simplistically explain that we inhabit a planet which is in rebellion, that we are part of a race living outside of God's will and that one consequence of that rebellion is sickness and death. God doesn't send it, nor does He will it. It is just a natural consequence of humanity's fallen state. Since we Christians are part of this race, we too sometimes suffer the consequences of that fallen state, even though we are personally committed to the doing of God's will and the coming of His kingdom.

Jesus defeated sickness and death through His own death and resurrection, but He has not yet destroyed it. That will happen at His second coming: "For he must reign until he has put all his enemies under his feet. The last enemy to be destroyed is death" (1 Cor. 15:25,26).

We can continue to ask why, we can constantly rail at God about the apparent injustice of life, the unfairness of it all, but that is just an exercise in futility.

Don't misunderstand me. I am not saying that we should never feel angry, never express our anger to God, never demand an explanation. Quite to the contrary, I believe that such expression is not only healthy, but necessary. It's part of the grief process; in order to get past our anger we often have to confess it honestly to God.

And we must come to the place that the "why" really doesn't matter, because in this life we only ". . . see through a glass, darkly. . . [we only] know in part. . ." (1 Cor. 13:12 KJV). If we will let Him, God will give us something better than answers or an explanation. He will give us unconditional trust!

Anyway, the real question isn't so much "Why?" but "Does God know, does He care?" And in response, all I can do is point to the cross. There He is — God's Son — bleeding and dying because He cares! The next time you are in the midst of a crisis and tempted to cry, "Lord, don't You care?" look to the cross. It says it all; it's all the answer we need!

Once we know that God cares, then we need the assurance that He is with us.

I truly believe that we can overcome any adversary, endure any hardship, if only we can know that we are not alone. Elaine St. Johns found peace in her time of trouble because that still, small voice assured her, "...lo, I am with you alway..." (Matt. 28:20 KJV). Hundreds of years ago, the psalmist had a similar experience, and he wrote: "Even though I walk through the valley of the shadow of death, I will fear no evil, *for you are with me;* your rod and your staff, they comfort me" (Ps. 23:4).

The key is God's presence — "...I will fear no evil, *for you are with me...*"

When I was just a boy of seven or eight, I awoke in the middle of the night and thought I saw a man rummaging through my closet. Fear froze me, paralyzed me, and I lay there trying not to breathe. For thirty seconds, a minute, maybe more, I couldn't do anything. Finally I managed a blood-curdling scream, and my father came barging into my bedroom. Of course, the intruder vanished, and Dad managed to assuage my fears and get me back to sleep.

Some time later I awoke again, and the intruder was back. This time he was standing directly over me. I tried to scream, but not a sound escaped my fear-constricted throat. I lay there, more afraid than I've ever been before or since. With a sudden lunge, I sat straight up in bed and screamed loud enough to wake the dead. Once more Dad came rushing to my rescue. Again the intruder disappeared.

Now that I'm older I'm convinced that intruder was just a figment of my overactive imagination, but you couldn't have convinced me of that back then. In fact, after the second experience, I refused to be comforted. My father's exhortations fell on deaf ears. Finally, in desperation, Dad sent my younger brother to sleep

151

with Mom and crawled into bed beside me. When he did, fear walked out.

That's still the answer to life's fears, whether great or small. We used to sing, "Every promise in the book is mine, every chapter, every verse, every line." It's as true today as it was then, and there's none more precious than the promise of God's presence.

At times our Father's presence is so real that we don't need anything else — not special people or special places. But those experiences are rare, and generally God manifests His presence through His people.

Maybe Alexander Irvine expressed it best in his novel, *My Lady of the Chimney Corner*. In this book, Irvine has "the lady" go comfort a neighbor whose boy lay dead:

"As gently as falls an autumn leaf, she laid her hand on Eliza's head: 'Ah, woman, God isn't a printed book to be carried aroun' by a man in fine clothes, not a cross danglin' at the watch chain of a priest. God takes a hand whenever he can find it, and just does what he like with it. Sometimes he takes a Bishop's hand and lays it on a child's head in benediction, and then he takes the hand of a doctor to relieve pain, the hand of a mother to guide a child, and sometimes he takes the hand of a poor old craither like me to give comfort to a neighbor. But they're all hands touched by His Spirit, and His Spirit is everywhere lukin' for hands to use."[4]

And finally, we must be sure that God will not allow our suffering to be wasted.

Somehow we are convinced that we can endure anything so long as we know it will count for something. That's one of the reasons families of the deceased, who are Christian, often encourage the minister to preach an "evangelistic message" at the funeral. Somehow their loss is made more bearable if they can feel it has furthered the Kingdom of God in some way. Unfortunately, this "need" can and does sometimes drive the bereaved to extreme explanations and even bizarre gestures. It need not do so, but it often does.

In Romans 8:28, the Apostle Paul states: "And we know that all things work together for good to them that love God, to them who are the called according to his purpose" (KJV). Now that's really all we need to know. Not *how* any particular thing works together for good, but just that it does! We don't even need to speculate about the ways, just take comfort in the fact that God is redeeming that situation or experience, making it work together for our eternal good!

Many years ago, I heard a story which made this truth come alive for me. It's a true story and tragic, about a minister whose son committed suicide. Ten days later, the minister entered the pulpit and announced his text. Under real duress he read Romans 8:28. Visibly struggling, he said:

"I cannot make my son's suicide fit into this passage. It's impossible for me to see how anything good can come out of it, but even in my pain-blinded state I realize that I only see in part and I only know in part. The scope of this verse is beyond me and somehow it supports me, enables me to go on living even though life doesn't seem to make any sense. Somehow I believe when all of life is over, when God has fully worked out His will, even my son's suicide will be woven into the final tapestry of His eternal design.

"It's like the mystery, the miracle of the shipyard. Almost every part of our great ocean-going vessels is made of steel and if you take any single part, be it a steel plate out of the hull or the huge rudder, and throw it into the ocean it will sink. But when the shipbuilders are finished, when the last plate has been riveted in place, when the last part has been bolted properly then that massive steel ship will float.

"Taken by itself my son's suicide is senseless. Throw it into the sea of Romans 8:28 and it sinks. But I believe that when the eternal shipbuilder is finally finished, when God has worked out His perfect design, even this senseless tragedy will somehow work to our eternal good!"

I am not suggesting, not even for a moment, that God causes or wills the capricious tragedies that come our way. Perhaps He allows them, but for certain He redeems them, He uses them for our eternal good. "Many are the afflictions of the righteous: but the Lord delivereth him out of them all" (Ps. 34:19). The very things that the enemy intended to destroy us, God redeems and uses as instruments for furthering His eternal purposes in our lives and in the kingdom. It's critically important that we believe this and commit ourselves and our situations to God; otherwise we will risk a life of bitterness and hurt.

"A few years ago," writes Arthur Gordon in *A Touch of Wonder*, "some friends of ours were given the heartbreaking news that their teenage son was going blind, that nothing could be done. Everyone was torn with pity for them, but they remained calm and uncomplaining. One night, as we left their house, I tried to express my admiration for their fortitude.

"I remember how the boy's father looked up at the stars. 'Well,' he said, 'it seems to me that we have three choices. We can curse life for doing this to us, and look for some way to express our grief and rage. Or we can grit our teeth and endure it. Or we can accept it. The first alternative is useless. The second is sterile and exhausting. The third is the only way.' "⁵

Acceptance. Now that's what I'm talking about. Not resignation which gives up and says, "Whatever will be, will be." But acceptance which keeps believing for a miracle even as it accepts the reality of present difficulty. Acceptance does not demand a predetermined conclusion, rather it leaves the nature of the miracle to the wisdom of God. It may come in the form of divine intervention in the circumstances of life. Or it may come as a miracle in our spirit, enabling us to experience peace and fulfillment while living in the most desperate straits.

Acceptance means that we stop fighting God, we stop blaming Him for life's hardships. In fact, it may mean that we go so far as to forgive Him for what has happened to us.

Theologically, I know that sounds insane. Who are we to forgive God? Who are we to presume that God needs forgiving?

Hear me out. We are not forgiving God because He has done something wrong, for He hasn't. Rather, we are forgiving Him in the sense that we have blamed Him, held Him responsible, and our feelings have alienated us from Him. When we "forgive" Him, we let go of those feelings — all of the hurt and anger, all of the bitterness and distrust. It means we stop working against His purposes in our life. Instead, we yield ourselves to Him, we work with Him. And, as a result, we experience His supernatural peace.

Frequently we are angry at God because things haven't turned out the way we expected. As a result, we often find ourselves not only battling life's vicissitudes, but life itself; we are at cross purposes with God.

Somewhere we picked up the mistaken idea that because we are Christians we have the right to a problem-free, pain-free life. Nothing could be further from the truth. Jesus told His disciples: ". . . In the world ye shall have tribulation: but be of good cheer; I have overcome the world" (John 16:33 KJV).

Once we realize this truth and get our expectations right, then acceptance — and the peace it produces — will come more naturally. Or as Annie Johnson Flint put it:

"God hath not promised
    Skies always blue,
Flower-strewn pathways
    All our lives through;
God hath not promised
    Sun without rain,
Joy without sorrow,
    Peace without pain.
But God hath promised
    Strength for the day,
Rest for the labor,
    Light for the way,

Grace for the trials,
    Help from above,
Unfailing sympathy,
    Undying love."[6]

That's the real strength of Christianity. Not that it makes us immune to life's difficulties, but that it gives us resources to deal with them redemptively. It enables us to be loving in the most hostile relationships, to find joy where others find only futility, and to experience peace even in the time of trouble.

Footnotes

1. Annie Johnson Flint, "HE GIVETH MORE GRACE," music by Hubert Mitchell (Lillenas Publishing Co., 1941, 1969).

2. Elaine St. Johns, quoted in *Dawnings: Finding God's Light in the Darkness,* edited by Phyllis Hobe (New York: Guideposts Associates, Inc., 1981) pp. 34, 37.

3. Ibid., p. 37.

4. Alexander Irvine, *My Lady of the Chimney Corner,* quoted in *Barefoot Days of the Soul,* by Maxie Dunnam (Waco: Word Books Publisher), pp. 114, 115.

5. Arthur Gordon, *A Touch of Wonder* (Old Tappan: Fleming H. Revell Company, 1984) p. 89.

6. Annie Johnson Flint, "What God Hath Promised," quoted in *Dawnings: Finding God's Light in the Darkness,* edited by Phyllis Hobe (Waco: Word Books Publisher, 1981), p. 40.

Chapter 8

THE GLORY OF LIFE

Joy is a many-splendored thing —
a phone call from an old friend,
a good book,
a second cup of coffee,
a warm fire on a winter night.
It's life's little pleasures,
autumn colors,
the season's first snow,
the sound of rain on a tin roof,
the pungent odor of a dusty barn
resurrecting childhood memories
of haylofts and hide 'n seek.

Joy is a many-splendored thing.
It's special moments like births and baptisms,
things that only happen once.
Your sixteenth birthday, turning twenty-one,
landing your first job, buying your own car,
seeing the Grand Canyon for the first time,
publishing your first book.
It's rare and tender moments —
getting married and making love,
giving birth, becoming a grandparent,
growing old with the one you love.

Joy is a many-splendored thing.
It's the rush of emotion
a mother feels at the moment of birth.
The bittersweet pleasure
of watching her child grow up
and start to school.
The excitement of your child's first date,
the tenderly poignant moment when you realize
she's truly in love,

that one day soon she will belong to another,
give birth to children of her own,
and become a mother.

Joy is a many-spendored thing —
a strange and wonderful mixture
   of love and laughter,
       pain and sorrow,
           life and death.
It's the comfort of friends
when you stand beside the open grave
of the one you've loved and lived with
   your whole life long.
It's the strength of scripture
   in the dark hour of unspeakable need.
It's the memory of His faithfulness,
   the promise of His presence.
Joy is a many-splendored thing.

Chapter 8

THE GLORY OF LIFE

"Recent archeological discoveries uncovered letters written by martyrs during the first three centuries following Christ. Just before death one saint penned, 'In a dark hole I have found cheerfulness; in a place of bitterness and death I have found rest. While others weep I have found laughter, where others fear I have found strength. Who would believe that in a state of misery I have had great pleasure; that in a lonely corner I have had glorious company, and in the hardest bonds perfect repose. All those things Jesus has granted me. He is with me, comforts me and fills me with joy. He drives bitterness from me and fills me with strength and consolation.' "[1]

I can't help contrasting that early believer and his testimony with most contemporary Christians. He was a victim of religious persecution, a prisoner facing death for his faith. Christians today, at least in America, enjoy religious freedom. The only persecution we are likely to suffer is a mild form of mockery.

This man's abode was a damp cell — a "dark hole," to use his words — while we live in comfortable homes. His companions were a motley bunch — hardened criminals, incorrigible, embittered, for the most part, by their lot in life. We, on the other hand, live and work with our peers. We have a spiritual and social network, a support system which provides both fellowship and encouragement.

In that most miserable state, he found joy. In our comfort, it often eludes us.

Don't misunderstand me, I am not suggesting that he "had great pleasure" because of his hardships. Or that we lack fulfillment because we are inundated with creature comforts and modern conveniences. It's not nearly that simple. In fact, there appears to be little or no connection between a person's circumstances and *true joy*.

"The eminent preacher Harold Bosley recalled a story out of the days of the Great Depression in the early 1930s. A panel of speakers including Clarence Darrow, the distinguished attorney and professed atheist, were addressing a meeting of people from Chicago's Southside — most of them black. The economic conditions were at their worst: money and jobs were scarce and Darrow used that fact to point out the plight of the black people. He summed up their woes, concluding, 'And yet you sing? No one can sing like you do! What do you have to sing about?' Quick as a flash, a lady in the congregation shouted, 'We got Jesus to sing about!' And her reponse was followed by many 'Amens' and 'Yeses' and 'That's rights.'

"Uncharacteristically, Darrow for once was stopped dead in his tracks. He had no response, for he was face to face with that which cannot be rationalized, hardly even talked about, in human terms — people who can sing through tears and above their fears because they walk with the one who strengthens them to do all things."[2]

Obviously, this kind of joy has something to do with being in right relationship with Jesus, but it's more than just being "born again." If that were all there was to it, then all believers would live in a constant state of euphoria. Unfortunately, that's not the case.

This joyfulness is a learned experience. At least it was for the Apostle Paul who wrote: "...I have *learned* the secret of being content in any and every situation, whether well fed or hungry, whether living in plenty or in want" (Phil. 4:12).

It's not theory with him, either, he's talking right out of his life experience. In fact, at the time he penned those words, he was in a Roman prison awaiting execution for his faith in the Lord Jesus Christ. Yet there's not so much as a hint of self-pity.

And it's not the first time Paul has put his life on the line either, for he writes:

"...I have worked much harder, been in prison more frequently, been flogged more severely, and been exposed to death again and again. Five times I received from the Jews the forty lashes minus one. Three times I was beaten with rods, once I was stoned, three times I was shipwrecked, I spent a night and a day in the open sea, I have been constantly on the move. I have been in danger from rivers, in danger from bandits, in danger from my own countrymen, in danger from Gentiles; in danger in the city, in danger in the country, in danger at sea; and in danger from false brothers. I have labored and toiled and have often gone without sleep; I have known hunger and thirst and have often gone without food; I have been cold and naked. Besides everything else, I face daily the pressure of my concern for all the churches."

2 Corinthians 11:23-28

Here's a man who has few, if any, of the amenities which most of us consider necessary if we are to be content. He has no home, no wife or family. His only earthly possessions are a cloak and some parchments. He is misunderstood and hated by his own countrymen, separated from his friends and in poor health — yet he is happy. Not with the superficial hilarity that often is mistaken for happiness, not that cheap imitation which is all sunshine and laughter, but real, honest-to-goodness joy, which is at least one part sorrow for every two parts joy — contentment.

What had he learned? What was the secret of his contentment?

It's nothing so simple as a single axiom, life is too complex for that. Rather it's a collage of wisdom collected through the years.

First, he was committed to a cause greater than himself. His whole life was devoted to the fulfillment of his divine call.

Secondly, he had a servant's heart. He didn't ask what people could do for him, but what he could do for them.

Thirdly, he had learned the value of relationships. He loved people rather than things.

Fourthly, he had learned how to give thanks. He had a deep appreciation for life. Rather than grieving over what he had lost, he gave thanks for what he had.

Finally, he had mastered the holy art of celebrating the ordinary. As a result, he experienced contentment in any and all circumstances.

Now let's consider these "secrets" one at a time.

Paul experienced a consistent joy, a deep-seated contentment, because he had made *a commitment to a cause greater than himself.*

From that moment on the road to Damascus, when he was confronted by the resurrected Christ, until the day outside of Rome when he laid his head on the executioner's block, Paul was consumed with a holy passion. He lived to take the Gospel to the Gentiles, to tell the glorious news of God's love, which manifested itself in Jesus Christ, to all those who had never heard. Nothing else mattered. All other concerns paled beside this holy obsession. No risk was too great, no sacrifice too costly, no hardship too severe, and no distance too far.

"...to live is Christ," he cries, expressing the consuming passion of his life, "and to die is gain" (Phil. 1:21).

This secret is not unique to Paul. If life is to be meaningful and fulfilling, for any of us, we must have a reason for living, something we believe in enough to die for it. Noted psychologist William James often said, "The only truly happy people I know are those who have found a cause to live for which is greater than themselves."

By the same token, the most unhappy people I know are those who have no better reason for living than the pursuit of pleasure or the quest for personal fulfillment. The scriptures give us a classic example of a man trapped in this very futility. He's familiar even to the most elementary Bible student. His name is Solomon, and he had everything — wealth, wisdom, worldwide recognition, and an ever-deepening weariness. Hear him as he laments the emptiness of life: "I have seen all the things that are done under the sun; all of them are meaningless, a chasing after the wind" (Eccl. 1:14).

Describing his unbridled pursuit of pleasure, he confesses, "I denied myself nothing my eyes desired; I refused my heart no pleasure...But that also proved to be meaningless" (Eccl. 2:10,1).

If Solomon were only another rich playboy, his emptiness would be easier to understand, but he isn't. He's the head of state, the King of Israel, an ambitious man who literally transformed those twelve nomadic tribes into a world power. His domestic programs made Israel the envy of all her neighbors. He undertook great projects and amassed enormous wealth, yet without experiencing personal fulfillment:

"...I built houses for myself and planted vineyards. I made gardens and parks and planted all kinds of fruit trees in them. I made reservoirs to water groves of flourishing trees...I amassed silver and gold for myself, and the treasure of kings and provinces. I acquired men and women singers, and a harem as well — the delights of the heart of man...Yet when I surveyed all that my hands had done and what I had toiled to achieve, everything was meaningless, a chasing after the wind; nothing was gained under the sun" (Eccl. 2:4-6,8,11).

What a contrast: the aged apostle, battle-scarred and bent, living out his days in a Roman cell, destined for death at the executioner's hand, yet he exults in the joy of the Lord. "I rejoice greatly in the Lord. . . for I have learned to be content whatever the circumstances. . . I have learned the secret of being content in any and every situation, whether well fed or hungry, whether living in plenty or in want" (Phil. 4:10-12).

Solomon, on the other hand, an aging king, resplendent in the trappings of wealth and power, known worldwide for his wisdom and his achievements, recognized as the most powerful man on earth, yet desperately unhappy. In frustration he writes, ". . . I hated life, because the work that is done under the sun was grievous to me. All of it is meaningless, a chasing after the wind" (Eccl. 2:17).

Paul found meaning and contentment under the most adverse circumstances, because he had *a reason for living, a cause greater than himself.* Solomon's life was empty and meaningless, in spite of all his achievements, because he lived only for himself, he had no higher goal than his own fulfillment.

If you're not content, not fulfilled, let me urge you to examine your commitments. Are you living only for yourself? Is there anything that you would willingly die for? That's the secret, isn't it? Finding something (or someone) for which you would gladly give your life.

Victor Frankl, the Austrian psychiatrist who developed the logotherapy approach to counseling, spent three years in Nazi concentration camps during World War II. In those death camps, millions of Jews were "exterminated" by the Nazis. Thousands more were subjected to "medical" experiments of the most hideous nature, and all inmates lived in unimaginably deprived conditions. Under such brutal and inhuman circumstances, death seemed a welcome escape, and many inmates chose it. They simply lost their will to live, and so they died. In fact, with the exception of one sister, all of Frankl's immediate family — parents, siblings, wife and children — perished during the war.

Frankl survived, and he helped others to survive, by realizing "...that it did not really matter what we expected from life, but rather what life expected from us."[3] He concluded that life expected him to serve his fellow inmates by providing an underground health system, including mental health.

"For example, he helped prevent two suicide attempts by asking the men what life asked of them. One of these men then chose to live for his child, and the other chose to live to complete a task, a series of scientific books. Frankl noted, therefore, that both human love and creative work can give meaning to life."[4]

If making a commitment to something other than one's own self could produce meaning, a reason to go on living, in such adverse circumstances as those found in the death camps, then surely it follows that it will work for us as well. Or as an anonymous writer put it:

"The Glory of Life is to love,
Not to be loved.
To give, not to get,
To serve, not to be served;
To be a strong hand in the dark to another
    in the time of need,
To be a cup of strength to any soul in a crisis
    of weakness.
This is to know The Glory of Life."[5]

That, I believe, sums up the second prerequisite for contentment: *A commitment "to serve, rather than to be served."* Jesus taught this principle both by word and deed:

"During supper, Jesus...rose from table, laid aside his garments, and taking a towel, tied it round him. Then he poured water into a basin, and began to wash his disciples' feet and to wipe them with the towel...

"After washing their feet and taking his garments again, he sat down. 'Do you understand what I have done for you?' he asked. 'You call me "Master" and "Lord", and rightly so, for that is what I am. Then if I, your Lord and Master, have washed your feet, you also ought to wash one another's feet. I have set you an example: you are to do as I have done for you. In very truth I tell you, a servant is not greater than his master, nor a messenger than the one who sent him. If you know this, happy are you if you act upon it.' "

John 13:3-5,12-17 NEB

That's a principle I learned early in my ministry, while I was still in my first pastorate. It was a difficult congregation, small and riddled with petty jealousies. I had served the church just over a year when things reached a boiling point.

In desperation I cried out to the Lord and, over a two- or three-week period, I became convinced that He was directing me to conduct an old-fashioned foot-washing service. That prospect made little or no sense to me, but the situation was desperate, and my inner promptings seemed to become stronger by the day, so I decided to "go for it."

The following Sunday morning I announced that the evening service would be "for men only." Immediately there was some uneasy murmuring and by the time I reached the parsonage, which was just next door to the church, the phone was ringing. It was Brother Hoover, an eighty-four-year-old man and a longtime member of the church. He informed me that his wife had been attending church with him for more than sixty years and that if she was not welcome in the service, then he wasn't coming either.

Without giving me a chance to reply, he hung up. I was sick at heart. The Hoovers were one of the few families in the church who weren't "opposing" me, and now I had offended them!

It was too late to change my mind, so, in spite of my misgivings, I went ahead with the service as planned. That evening there were nine men in attendance, sitting on metal folding chairs, facing each other. They sat quietly, occasionally glancing toward the communion table where I stood. Finally I started the service by instructing the men to remove their shoes and socks. They looked at each other as if to say, "This kid (I was only twenty-one at the time) has really lost his mind this time." Still, they did as I requested and in a matter of minutes we had two rows of barefoot men facing each other.

While the men were removing their shoes and socks, I took off my coat and rolled up my shirt sleeves. Now, picking up a basin of water and a towel, I turned and faced them.

"Some of you feel I've played favorites, that I haven't ministered to your families as I should. You probably have some justification for your feelings too. But I want you to know that any time I wronged you, I did it ignorantly, out of inexperience, never maliciously. As a demonstration of my sincere desire to serve you, in any way, great or small, I'm going to wash your feet."

Again there was some uneasy murmuring, but I ignored it and knelt before the nearest man. Before I washed his feet, I apologized for any wrong I had done him and asked his forgiveness. Then I washed his feet as a demonstration of my willingness to serve him and his family in Jesus' name. I repeated that act eight more times, until I had apologized specifically to every man present and had washed the feet of all in attendance.

During that simple ritual, something almost miraculous took place, in their hearts and in mine. By taking a towel and a basin of water, by getting down on my knees, by washing their feet and apologizing, I had disarmed those men. I had taken the fuse out of the time bomb of their anger. When I made myself vulnerable, when I placed myself in their hands, at their mercy, I appealed to all the love and goodness in their hearts. The spiritual dictator making demands and giving instructions was gone, and in his place was a non-threatening servant.

And that experience changed me too, radically, from the inside out. Until that service, I had always thought of ministers, especially evangelists, as "sanctified celebrities." We were the stars, the headliners, and the Church existed to benefit us.

I'm not sure where I got that mistaken idea (it was before the time of televangelists, so I can't blame my misconception on their celebrity status). Still that false idea was there. With an attitude like that, I couldn't help but notice every slight, however insignificant. As a result, I was constantly unhappy. I felt that I wasn't appreciated, that my needs weren't being met.

What was God's answer for my self-serving attitude? A basin of water and a towel. "...if I, your Lord and Master, have washed your feet, you also ought to wash one another's feet...*If you know this, happy are you if you act upon it.*"

Of course, He wasn't just talking about washing feet. This is an attitude, a way of living, a willingness to give yourself in loving service to others, in all ways, in even the most mundane manner, especially if it can be done without attracting notice. "...and your Father, who sees what is done in secret, will reward you" (Matt. 6:18). The first way in which He rewards us, I might add, is with renewal, contentment, inner joy!

Ann Kiemel Anderson writes, "something...that has helped me in depression is to move beyond my pain & reach out to someone else. i remember one day feeling so depressed i could hardly roll over in bed. there was no energy left in me for anything. somehow, i wanted to stay under the covers & just die.

"with sheer, gut determination, i rolled out of bed. put clothes on my body with every thread of strength i could muster. stopped at a grocery store & bought two sacks full for a lonely, old widower. i sang to him, & visited with him, & left the groceries on his kitchen table. there were a couple other people i thought of. one, a teen-age boy who was so socially crippled. picking up two cokes, i sat on the front steps with him & let him tell me his problems.

"it was dark by the time i returned home. nothing had changed in my life. all the problems still existed. but i was lighthearted. the terrible weight of darkness & weariness was gone. i saw a streak of hope stretch across the sky. new energy surged in me.

"depression can be so selfish, so crippling. give your life away to others, over & over & over, & the black, dark places will become lighter. refuse, stubbornly, to let it block out the needs of others, to encase you in a tunnel of self-doubt & greed."[6]

Ann's antidote for depression was to serve others. She forgot her needs by focusing on theirs! Try it and I believe you will be pleasantly surprised. Seek for joy, and you will never find it. Give it away to others, and it will find you. It works every time!

The third secret Paul learned about contentment, in any and all circumstances, was to appreciate *the value of friendship*. You cannot read his epistles without sensing his deep commitment to his friends and co-workers, and theirs to him. Often they walked with him through difficulties and danger, sometimes even risking their own lives, and he wasn't one to forget that. Consider his letter to his friends in the Corinthian church:

". . . I have said before that you have such a place in our hearts that we would live or die with you. I have great confidence in you; I take great pride in you. I am greatly encouraged; in all our troubles my joy knows no bounds.

"For when we came into Macedonia, this body of ours had no rest, but we were harassed at every turn — conflicts on the outside, fears within. But God, who comforts the downcast, comforted us by the coming of Titus, and not only by his coming but also by the comfort you had given him. He told us about your longing for me, your deep sorrow, your ardent concern for me, so that my joy was greater than ever."

2 Corinthians 7:3-7

Several years ago, more than fifteen now, I was passing through a difficult time in my life. Part of it was my fault, but at the time I couldn't see that. I simply felt betrayed, wounded by the church I had chosen to serve, rejected and misunderstood by my peers. It was a complicated situation, and there is nothing to be gained by delving into the painful details. Suffice it to say that, were it not for some special friends, two in particular, I probably would not be in the ministry today.

The first is Darrel Madsen, who is now a District Superintendent, but at the time he was still a pastor. Following a painful misunderstanding, I suddenly found myself without a place to minister, wondering if there was really any place for me in the organized Church. I was hurt, angry, probably even a little bitter, really not in much condition to minister effectively. Still, Pastor Madsen invited me to join his staff as a kind of adjunct associate. I readily accepted, so desperate was I to be needed and appreciated.

The weeks I spent with him were healing, and without his stubborn love, I shudder to think of what might have become of my ministry. Across the years, he and his wife Barbara have again and again affirmed me. When my first book was published, he invited me to preach in his church (a very large and important one, I might add) and hosted a reception in my honor. Before anyone else recognized me as a retreat speaker, he invited me to lead the annual retreat for his church and recommended my ministry to others. He believed in me and helped me to believe in myself. I guess that says it all!

Following my brief time on his staff, I seemed to do all right for a while, then the invitations to minister dried up again. In desperation I turned to odd jobs to provide, at least in some measure, for my wife and baby daughter. I stacked hay in Colorado, worked as a longshoreman at the Port of Houston, drove a grain truck during harvest, and finally ended up with a bit part in a movie being filmed at Buckskin Joe, just outside of Canon City, Colorado. It was a miserable existence, and once more I was tempted to turn my back on the ministry, and on God too.

For several weeks I lived in an ever-deepening depression. I covered it pretty well, but on the inside I felt as though I was dying. I loved God, but I didn't feel I could trust Him. I loved the ministry, but there didn't seem to be any place for me. I guess I felt betrayed, yet at the same time I knew there was disobedience in my own heart.

The conflict became almost debilitating before I finally surrendered. Once again I turned to some special friends. This time it was Bob and Diana.

As I thought about them, I was almost overwhelmed. They were the first two converts of our ministry in Holly, Colorado. Many was the time Bob would call and say, "Diana has just baked a loaf of bread and we've got a bottle of grape juice. Why don't you and Brenda come out and have Communion with us?" Suddenly I wanted that, more than anything. I wanted that special relationship, with them, and with Jesus.

Then and there, I made a decision. I was going to find them, and in the safety of their love I was going to recommit my life to the Lord. Without a word to anyone, I just walked off the movie set where I was working. I drove to Canon City, picked up Brenda and our daughter Leah, and headed for Kansas.

Bob and Diana, it turned out, were working on a farm in the southwestern part of the state. After driving for most of the day and making a half-dozen phone calls, we finally located them. Though they hadn't heard from us in over two years, they were delighted when we showed up. It was as if we had never been apart.

On Saturday I bought a bottle of grape juice and I asked Diana if she would bake some bread. After we got the kids to bed, we gathered around the scarred coffee table in their living room, just like old times, only now our roles were reversed. Many was the time I had heard Bob's confession, now he heard mine. Many was the time I had cried and prayed with the two of them, now they wept and prayed with me.

I poured out my heart, I confessed everything — my hurt, my bitterness, even how close I had come to losing my faith. There were a lot of tears then, and a lot of love, and that old farmhouse became a holy place, a sanctuary. We broke bread together, celebrated Holy Communion, and this broken man was made whole again.

The circumstances of my life didn't suddenly change. I still didn't have a place to preach, or a way of providing for my family, but those things seemed somehow inconsequential, especially in the light of the holy thing which had just happened in my life. I was forgiven, I was among friends, I was back home at last, where I belonged. With God, my family, and my friends I could face anything.

That is the heart of things, isn't it? — special friends! With them we can be content whatever the circumstances of our lives. In times of sorrow, they comfort us; in times of weakness, they strengthen us; and in times of success, they celebrate with us. It's true — friendship does multiply our joy, even as it divides our sorrows!

And it's not only what friends can do for us in our moment of weakness, but what we can do for them as well, what happens when our lives merge in Jesus, however brief that may be.

"Once when I was preaching in Pueblo, Colorado, the pastor and I went to visit a woman in the psychiatric ward of a local hospital. We talked with her for a few minutes and then the pastor prayed. As he finished praying, I felt a deep compassion for her, so I reached out and took her hand and began to pray. Deep inside of me I could feel the glacier of my personal aloneness begin to break up. As I finished praying, there was an exhilarated sense of communication. We stood there looking at each other and both of us knew something had happened. In that moment I felt more at one with the human race than I ever had before."[7]

The fourth secret of contentment is *a thankful heart.*

THE GLORY OF LIFE

Paul exhorts us: "Rejoice in the Lord always. I will say it again: Rejoice!...whatever is true, whatever is noble, whatever is right, whatever is pure, whatever is lovely, whatever is admirable — if anything is excellent or praiseworthy — think about such things...And the peace of God, which transcends all understanding, will guard your hearts and your minds in Christ Jesus" (Phil. 4:4,8,7).

No matter how bad the situation, there is always something to be thankful for. If we focus on that, rather than on our loss, we will discover joy, even in the midst of the most despairing circumstances.

Maxie Dunnam, writing in *The Communicator's Commentary Volume 8*, shares the story of his dear friend and fellow pastor, Doyle Masters, who was stricken with cancer in November 1978. After the doctor told him the cancer was inoperable, Masters wrote an open letter to his congregation in which he focused on what remained to him rather than on what had been taken away. As a result, his letter, and his life, fairly sing with joy. He writes, in part:

"The options open to me medically are minimal and at best do not promise renewed energy nor longevity. The other option is to turn this over to God in faith for His healing and ultimate will. This we have been directed to do by God after much prayer and spiritual surrender. What the future holds we do not know, but we know God holds it....

"These past few days have rolled over us like an avalanche, leaving in their wake some central certainties which make up my Thanksgiving list. Out of the dark night of the soul has come the sunlight of God's love. I am thankful for God who is real and personal, for a Christ who is present in power, and for the Holy Spirit who is by our side in every struggle.

"My gratitude overflows for a faith that is unwavering in the face of seemingly unsurmountable obstacles, and for the personal practice of prayer that brings all God's promises to bear in any situation. . . .

"My Thanksgiving list is made this year not from what I have but from who has me — a God who is able to do exceedingly abundantly above all I ask or think."[8]

This is not a new revelation, still I never cease to be amazed by its transforming power. In fact, I recently had opportunity again to watch, almost in awe, as it worked its quiet miracle.

I was called upon to minister to a family in our church whose thirty-two-year-old son had been killed in an automobile accident. When I arrived, his mother was almost beside herself with grief. For the better part of an hour, maybe longer, I simply listened with love as she alternately poured out her anguish and then her anger.

Finally it seemed appropriate to speak; in fact, she was demanding an answer, some kind of explanation which would make some sense out of this otherwise senseless tragedy. Of course, such an answer doesn't exist, but I was able to help relieve the totality of her grief by helping her remember what she had (thirty-two years of happy memories) rather than what she had lost (a beloved son).

Gently I encouraged her to remember the rush of emotion that had swept over her when the doctor told her that she had given birth to a healthy baby boy.

"Remember," I urged, "the warmth that you felt when you nursed him, the peace as he lay sleeping, the excitement of his first steps. And his first day at school, his graduation, and his wedding day."

With an effort, she began to reminisce, to recall the love and the laughter they had shared. As she did, the awful pain of her grief gave way, just a little, to the joy of their shared past. She was still undone by the magnitude of her loss, and well she might be, but at least her grief was now tempered with memories of the good times she and her beloved son had shared. And that's important, for pain and loss have a way of demanding our attention; they focus all our thoughts on the tragedy, leaving us overwhelmed and fearful.

By an act of our will, we can turn our thoughts to more uplifting things. As we do, we can make peace with our pain.

I'm not talking about denial, but perspective. Our loss is real, as is our grief, but so are the memories we cherish, and the sunshine, and God. More and more I am realizing that if we can reach back and get some of the joy of yesterday, we will discover a sense of peace, even contentment, regardless of how grueling the present circumstances.

Which brings us to the final "secret" of contentment: *the ability to celebrate the ordinary.*

"One of the most tragic things I know about human nature," said Dale Carnegie, "is that all of us tend to put off living. We are all dreaming of some magical rose garden over the horizon — instead of enjoying the roses that are blooming outside our windows today."[9]

As a consequence of our "far-sightedness," we miss life. It passes us by while we are waiting for something extraordinary or unusual to happen.

Or we try too hard to make happiness "happen," and end up like Will Durant, who lost happiness — at least for a while. He writes:

"(For) many years I lost happiness. I sought it in knowledge, and found disillusionment. I sought it in writing, and found a weariness of the flesh. I sought it in travel, and my feet tired on the way. I sought it in wealth, and I found discord and worriment.

"And then one day, at a little station out on a wooded cliff near the sea, I saw a woman waiting in a tiny car, with a child asleep in her arms. A man alighted from a train, walked to her quickly, embraced her, and kissed the child gently, careful lest he should awaken it. They drove off together to some modest home among the fields; and it seemed to me that happiness was with them.

"Today I have neglected my writing. The voice of a little girl calling to me, 'Come out and play,' drew me from my papers and my books. Was it not the final purpose of my toil that I should be free to frolic with her, and spend unharassed hours with the one who had given her to me? And so we walked and ran and laughed together, and fell in the tall grass, and hid among the trees; and I was young again.

"Now it is evening; while I write, I hear the child's breathing as she sleeps in her cozy bed. And I know that I have found what I sought. I perceived that if I will do as well as I can the tasks for which life has made me, I shall find fulfillment, and a quiet lane of happiness for many years."[10]

Or as James M. Barrie wrote in "Little Privileges":

"Happiness is the art of finding joy and
    satisfaction in the little privileges of life:
a quiet hour in the sun instead of a far-away
    journey;
a little outing in the nearby woods instead
    of long trips away;
an hour with a friend instead of an
    extended visit with relatives,
a few pages of a book instead of hours of
    reading at a time,
a flash of sunset, a single beautiful flower, a
    passing smile, a kindly word, a little gift
    bestowed anonymously, a little
    thoughtfulness here and there as the
    days slip by.
Those who bring sunshine into the lives of
    others cannot keep it from themselves."[11]

Truly ". . . godliness with contentment is great gain" (1 Tim. 6:6) — the glory of life!

Footnotes

1. Charles Hembree, *Pocket of Pebbles* (Grand Rapids: Baker Book House, 1969), p. 33.

2. Maxie D. Dunnam, *The Communicator's Commentary Volume 8 Galatians, Ephesians, Philippians, Colossians, Philemon* (Waco: Word Books Publisher, 1982), pp. 320, 321.

3. Victor Frankl, *Man's Search for Meaning* (New York: Pocket Books, 1963), p. 122.

4. Paul R. Welter, Ed.D., *Counseling and the Search for Meaning* (Waco: Word Books Publisher, 1987), p. 53.

5. "True Glory," author unknown, quoted in *Dawnings: Finding God's Light in the Darkness*, edited by Phyllis Hobe (New York: Guideposts Associates, Inc., 1981), p. 202.

6. Ann Kiemel Anderson and Jan Kiemel Ream, *Struggling for Wholeness* (Nashville: Oliver-Nelson Books, 1986), p. 99.

7. Richard Exley, *The Painted Parable* (New York: Vantage Press, 1978), p. 89.

8. Dunnam, p. 321.

9. Dale Carneige, quoted in *Dawnings, Finding God's Light in the Darkness*, edited by Phyllis Hobe (New York: Guideposts Associates, Inc., 1981) p. 196.

10. Will Durant, quoted in *Dawnings: Finding God's Light in the Darkness*, edited by Phyllis Hobe (New York: Guideposts Associates, Inc., 1981), pp. 204,205.

11. James M. Barrie, quoted in *Dawnings: Finding God's Light in the Darkness*, edited by Phyllis Hobe (New York: Guideposts Associates, Inc., 1981) p. 196.

Chapter 9

NO GREATER LOVE

Lord,
Love is a pretty common theme.
We hear it all the time...
      true love,
         tough love,
            free love,
    a mother's love,
         even unconditional love.

Yet real love,
Your kind of love,
the kind of love the Bible talks about,
is a rare commodity indeed.
It's more than moonlight and music,
more than romantic sentiment,
more than sexual desire
or an emotional high.
Your love is the real thing!

Yet I'm sure it doesn't come easy,
even for You.
Faced with our littleness,
    our sinfulness,
        our selfishness,
           and our hard-heartedness,
even Your love must be hard pressed at times.

It's a choice, isn't it?
    not a feeling,
        but a discipline, an act of the will!
You choose to love us,
    to see our possibilities,
        to believe in us,
           even when we can't believe in ourselves.

I want to love like that,
but I can't,
at least not without Your help.
I'm only good at love
when it makes me feel good,
and that's not really love at all.
This unconditional love,
this real love, is beyond me.
Still, if You can keep loving me.
just a little longer,
maybe I can learn to be a holy lover too.
Amen.

Chapter 9

NO GREATER LOVE

My first remembrance of unconditional love occurred when I was only nine. It was a strange mixture of joy and sorrow. Sometime in the middle of the night, Mother went into labor. Dad took her to the hospital after bringing Grandma Exley to stay with my two brothers and me.

For the next two and a half days, Mother struggled to give birth to her fourth child. She succeeded only after the doctor belatedly decided to perform a cesarean section. I was too young to understand any of this at the time, but I can remember the laughter and cheers when Grandma told us we had a baby sister. In minutes we were announcing it to the neighborhood.

Some time later, Dad came home and gathered the three of us around him. He was bowed with weariness and grief and painful news. Yes, Mother did give birth to a daughter, our long-awaited sister, but things didn't look good. She was born with an enlarged head and wasn't expected to live long. Even if she did live, she would never be normal.

Tears were running down Dad's cheeks when he finished and I seemed to be smothering, I couldn't get my breath. I sat there numbly for a minute more, then I burst off the couch and ran through the dining room and kitchen, choking on my sobs. The screen door slammed against the house with a frightful racket as I flung it open and stumbled down the back steps toward the garage.

For the better part of the next hour, I lay with my face buried in the dirt floor. Great heaving sobs convulsed my small frame and it seemed everything in the universe withdrew, leaving me alone with my pain. The dusty floor mingled with my tears, becoming mud, and I pounded my fists into the ground until I had no strength left. After a long while, my grief seemed to have exhausted itself, leaving me with a hollow feeling in the pit of my stomach.

I think I accepted Carolyn's death that afternoon, though it wasn't to become a reality for almost three months. The intervening weeks were filled with several crises. Like the time Dad and Aunt Elsie made a flying trip to the children's hospital in Denver. When they arrived, Carolyn was critical, at the point of death. The doctors were able to stabilize her condition and, after she had spent some days in the hospital, we brought her home for the last time.

What does all of this have to do with love? I'm coming to that.

Carolyn's condition was pitiful. That's the kindest way I can put it. Undoubtedly, she seemed repulsive to others, but never to us. Vaguely I can remember Mother placing Carolyn in my lap, as I sat in the armchair, and watching with a painful love as I fed her a few ounces of formula.

It seemed each day brought some new disappointment. Soon we realized that Carolyn was both blind and deaf, and her head, larger than the rest of her tiny body at birth, became increasingly disproportionate. With a pain that lingers still, I remember watching Mother bathe Carolyn tenderly, then carefully measure her head to see if, by some miracle, it was any smaller. It never was. Mama would bite her lip then, while tears ran down her cheeks as she carefully put away the cloth tape measure.

The doctors suggested that Carolyn be placed permanently in the children's hospital in Denver where she could receive better care. My folks wanted to know if that would improve her life expectancy and if she would be more comfortable in the hospital. Not appreciably, the doctors acknowledged, but it would be less stressful on the family.

Mother and Dad thanked them for their concern, but they never really considered their recommendation. Carolyn wasn't an inconvenience to be disposed of in the most humanitarian fashion. She was their baby, a member of the family. If her condition required special care, then they would provide it. Their love was like that — unconditional! Somehow it made that unlovely child lovely, at least to us.

As I think about it now, I am almost in awe. Where does that kind of love come from? Before you conclude that it is instinctive to a parent, let me remind you that history is filled with tragic examples of parental cruelty. In fact, it was an accepted way of life in the ancient world where parents practiced the exposure of children:

"The unwanted child was simply thrown out like refuse. Hilarion writes to his wife Alis in I B.C. with the strangest mixture of love and callousness: 'Hilarion to his wife Alis, warmest greetings. . . I want you to know that we are still in Alexandria. Don't worry if, when they all go home, I stay on in Alexandria. I beg and entreat you, take care of the little child; and, as soon as we get our pay, I will send it up to you. If — good luck to you! — you bear a child, if it is a boy, let it live; if it is a girl, throw it out. You told Aphrodisias to tell me, "Don't forget me." How can I possibly forget you. Don't worry.'

"The exposure of an unwanted child was normal routine. In Stobaeus (Eclogues 75) there is a saying: 'The poor man raises his sons, but the daughters, if one is poor, we expose.'

"An exposed child might be picked up and trained for the brothels, or, worse, it might be deliberately maimed, and then used by some professional beggar to awaken the sympathy and extract alms of the passers-by.

"The child who was weak or sickly or ill-formed had little chance of survival. In the *Republic* (460 B.C.) Plato insists that only children of better unions must be kept, and any defective child must be done away with. 'Let there be a law,' says Aristotle, 'that no deformed child shall be reared' (Politics 7. 14. 10). Even Seneca lays it down: 'Mad dogs we knock on the head; the fierce and savage ox we slay; sickly sheep we put to the knife to keep them from infecting the flock; unnatural progeny we destroy; we drown even children who at birth are weakly and abnormal. It is not anger but reason which separates the harmful from the sound' (On Anger, 1. 15. 2)."[1]

Even though that's ancient history, we dare not smugly dismiss it. While the exposure of children is no longer socially acceptable, we do have our own ways of dealing with the unwanted — abuse and abortion.

In the United States alone, there are at least one million cases of child abuse each year, and many experts believe that there may actually be as many as six million incidents annually.[2]

"Every year two thousand children die from child abuse (some studies estimate as many as six thousand). Ten percent of emergency room visits by children are due to inflicted injuries. One study estimates fifteen of every one hundred children are abused at least five times annually. (In fact) more children under age five die from injuries inflicted by their parents than from tuberculosis, whooping cough, polio, measles, diabetes, rheumatic fever and appendicitis combined."[3]

And child abuse is minuscule compared to abortions.

"Each day in our country over 4000 human lives are ended by abortion. The numbers continue to multiply and already in cities like New York and Washington, D.C., there are more life ending abortions than live births."[4]

President Reagan said, in his address to the National Religious Broadcaster's convention in January 1984, "Fifteen million children will never laugh, never sing, never know the joy of human love. . ." Since that time, another estimated six million babies have been aborted, bringing the gruesome total to twenty-one million.

Such numbers defy the imagination, so let me try to put the magnitude of this atrocity into perspective. In the Revolutionary War, America suffered 25,324 fatalities. In the Civil War, there were 498,332 recorded deaths. In World War I, 116,516 American servicemen were killed; in World War II, 545,108; in the Korean War, 54,246; and in the Vietnam conflict, 56,555. That makes the total war dead of the United States 1,296,001, or about 1/20 of the number of deaths by abortion.[5]

Of course, humanity's cruelty is not reserved just for the young or the unborn. "In the Roman world," writes noted scholar William Barclay, "life was merciless especially to the slave and to the child. The slave, as Aristotle said (Nicomachean Ethics 8. 11. 6) was no different from a living tool, and what consideration can a tool receive? A master could, and did, kill his slave, as when Vedius Pollio flung his slave to the savage lampreys in the fishpool of his courtyard, because he had stumbled and broken a goblet (Pliny, Natural History 9. 23)."[6]

"Sir Henry Holland, the famous medical missionary from Quetta, whose work on eye troubles is world famous, tells how sometimes a patient would be brought in, in whom the trouble was so far advanced that his eyes were beyond the help of surgery. When he had to break news like that to a patient, the bystanders would roar with laughter, and tell the patient to be gone and not to be a nuisance to the doctor. Sympathy was unknown."[7]

And lest you be tempted to think that such cruelty is the particular domain of the pagan world or times past, let me remind you of the devastating effect terminal illness has on marriage and the family in our own modern Western civilization. Some researchers report a 70 percent breakup rate when one marriage partner has a terminal illness; the tensions simply prove unbearable.

Philip Yancey, author of *Where is God When It Hurts?*, tells of a thirty-seven-year-old friend who discovered he had one of the rarest, most severe forms of cancer. In medical history, only twenty-seven people were known to have been treated for this precise form of cancer. The other twenty-six patients were all dead.

At his friend's request, Philip began accompanying him to a therapy group which met at a nearby hospital. The group consisted of people who were dying, most of them were in their thirties.

Yancey writes, "I was most affected by the one elderly person in the room, a handsome, gray-haired woman with the broad, bony face of an Eastern European immigrant. She expressed her loneliness in simple sentences veiled in a thick accent. We asked if she had any family. An only son was trying to get emergency leave from the air force in Germany. And her husband? She swallowed hard a few times and then said, 'He came to see me just once. I was in the hospital. He brought me my bathrobe and a few things. The doctor stood in the hallway and told him about my leukemia.' Her voice started to crack, and she dabbed at her eyes before continuing. 'He went home that night, packed up all his things, and left. I never saw him again.'

" 'How long had you been married?' I asked.

"Several people in the group gasped aloud at her answer: 'Thirty-seven years.' "[8]

Yancy concludes with this painful observation. "In this group of thirty people, no marriages remained intact longer than two years — including my friend Jim's."[9]

What's the point in all of this? Apparently we human beings have a limited capacity for love apart from the love of God manifest in Jesus Christ. Without the influence of His love, humanity's cruelty and lovelessness knows no limit. Only when an individual, or a society, allows God to love them are they capable of expressing real selfless love.

That's not to say that every "born-again" believer is an unselfish lover, or that a "Christian" society is totally free of racism, intolerance, and injustice. But when the true Church, even with all its imperfections, is compared to the unchurched, there is a marked difference in the quality of its relationships and its concern for the world. This is equally true when a "Christian" nation is compared to those not founded on the Judeo-Christian ethic.

Where do we go from here? That depends on whether we are content with the world as it is; whether we are content with our life. If you are not satisfied with things as they are, if you have caught a glimpse of what the world can be, then let me challenge you to let God love you.

That's probably not what you expected. The usual exhortation is to become more involved, more loving. Believe, me, there is a time for that, but not yet. First we must let God love us, and that's not as easy as it sounds. In fact, the more I think about it, the more convinced I become that most of the world is afraid to let God love them.

Donald Macleod, formerly the Professor of Preaching and Worship at Princeton Theological Seminary, explains it like this: "People who are satisfied with the slogan, 'Anything goes,' will avoid the church [God's love] because it confronts them with facts that disturb and irritate them. They do not want to be reminded of the claims of truth, duty, love to God, and charity toward others. It is much easier to live by a philosophy of positive thinking that makes no demand beyond saying every morning before the mirror: 'Every day and in every way I am getting better and better.' It is much easier to talk about love of the synthetic kind which is paraded by the soap operas on the national television networks than it is to gaze on real love which dies on a cross. In church you and I come up against real virtues and God asks: 'What is your personal relationship to these?' In church we encounter the eternal cleavage between right and wrong, love and hate, truth and falsehood."[10]

I can identify with that. It is impossible to let God love us and remain the way we are. Let down your defenses for just a moment, crack your life open just the tiniest bit, and there it is, God's love, silhouetted against the dark sky of human history, against all of the faults and failures, against all of humanity's wickedness and wandering. There it is — the cross! God dressed in the garments of human flesh, bleeding and dying, courting our love.

But who can bear to look on love like that? We are tempted to cover our eyes, to look the other way, to pretend that we haven't seen. It's too late. We have looked, and we have seen, and now we can never be the same. Love so terrible and so grand draws us like iron filings to a magnet. We are caught up into the very bosom of God, taken into His great heart.

How ragged and self-serving our ambitions seem in the light of such love. How tragic the pettiness and littleness of our lives; how cold and hard our hearts. Yet there is no condemnation here, only love; liberating love, redeeming love. He heals our hurts, rights the old wrongs, and strangely warms our cold hearts. Soon our lives pulsate with the eternal reality of His divine love.

You may be wondering, "Can God love me like that with all my inadequacies?" Believe me, He can and He does!

I can almost hear God say, "I don't love you because I'm a God of love, though I am. I don't love you because that's what I do best, though it is. I don't even love you because I'm supposed to, though I am. I love you because there's something about you that touches My heart!"

Think about that for a minute — there's something about you that touches His heart! That's hard to believe, isn't it?

What is there for God to love in the woman who has gone through three divorces and whose self-image is so poor that she is driven to seek masculine companionship at any cost? Is there really any goodness beneath the bitter cynicism her brittle smile can never quite mask? And what about the insensitive husband who seems indifferent to the needs of his wife and children? Or the irritating co-worker? Is there any loveliness in her?

To each of these people, and to us, God says, "There's just something about you that touches My heart!"

Beneath our obnoxious behavior, cleverly camouflaged by our willfulness, God sees something of Himself. Only a shadow perhaps, but undeniable just the same. His eternal likeness is there, planted deep in the soil of our soul, waiting only for the sunshine of His love to cause it to spring forth, a tender plant of rare beauty.

Defensiveness and self-depreciation often cause us to act in the most unloving ways, but He sees beyond our outrageous behavior. He knows that often when we need love in the worst way, we act the most unlovable. Still He loves us!

Across the years, I've witnessed God's holy love at work in some of the most unlikely people, and in the most unlikely ways, but none more unlikely than in the case of Sterling. I first met him when he came to my office for pastoral counseling. He was only a few days removed from the county jail and newly converted. Haltingly he told me his story.

He never knew his father, and his mother abandoned him when he was just a small boy. A kindly aunt took him in and reared him as her own. Still, her love could not heal the wound his parents' rejection had inflicted. By the time he was fourteen, he was a confirmed alcoholic and constantly in trouble with the authorities.

His incorrigible behavior finally resulted in his being sent to reform school. Unfortunately, that intensified his anger and bitterness, and upon his release he immediately returned to his antisocial behavior. Soon he was serving a sentence in the state penitentiary, then another.

When he came to see me, he was out on bail awaiting trial for allegedly raping his sixteen-year-old stepdaughter. While in the county jail, he had started reading the Bible and was born again. Now he wanted to know if he could become part of our church. I assured him that he could, and soon he was deeply involved in the life of our fellowship including a growth group which I led once a week. I can still remember the night he told us that he finally felt loved, for the first time in his life, by God and by the group.

Some weeks later, Sterling returned to my office, deeply agitated.

"Pastor," he said, "my trial starts in just a few days and then everyone will know what I'm accused of."

He stumbled to a halt and the silence became almost unbearable before he finally spoke again.

"I'm scared, really scared. Not so much of prison, I've been there before, but of being rejected by my church. I'm afraid they won't have anything more to do with me when they realize I'm on trial for rape."

I hastened to assure him that the church would stand with him, and he seemed a little comforted when he left. After he was gone though, I began to have some serious doubts of my own. Rape is a heinous crime, especially when it involves children, and ours was a young congregation with several familes having daughters. My own daughter was only seven, and I couldn't help but be concerned for her.

Sterling was my friend, he shared meals with our family, I knew him personally; yet I still had moments when I was assailed with misgivings. As I thought about it, I concluded that Sterling's concern was probably more legitimate than I had let on.

The following Sunday evening, at the conclusion of the service, I felt impressed to share Sterling's story with the congregation. Better to hear it from me, I reasoned, than to read about it in the newspaper. As I spoke, a somber silence settled over the congregation and I began to wonder if I had made a mistake. I finished by saying, "I assured Sterling that old things had passed away and that everything was made new when he was born again and that, as far as we were concerned, the past is under the blood of Jesus."

For what seemed a long time, no one moved and Sterling, sitting near the front, seemed to shrink within himself as it appeared that his worst fears were about to be realized. Then Mary got up and started toward him.

I didn't know whether to be encouraged or not; I wasn't sure what she would do. As a child, Mary had been sexually molested, and at the age of eighteen she became pregnant after being raped. For years, anger and fear haunted her, and she constantly contended with her hatred for men.

She stopped in front of Sterling, and I held my breath. Slowly she reached down and took his hand.

"Jesus loves you and so do we." Her voice cracked as a wave of emotion washed over her. "The past doesn't matter. You're forgiven. We're family!"

By now Sterling was crying and there was hardly a dry eye in the place. Suddenly it seemed that everyone was talking at once and crowding around Sterling to affirm their love and support. It was one of those rare and tender moments when love, God's love, triumphed over the harsh realities of human weakness.

Surely God must have been proud of that little church, at least for one brief moment, as we let His love shine through us.

I share Sterling's story because if God could find value in a man with a "rap sheet" as long as his arm, a man accused of raping his own sixteen-year-old stepdaughter, then surely you must realize that God loves you too, regardless of your sinfulness.

The Apostle Paul writes:

"Even though I was once a blasphemer and a persecutor and a violent man, I was shown mercy because I acted in ignorance and unbelief. The grace of our Lord was poured out on me abundantly, along with the faith and love that are in Christ Jesus.

"Here is a trustworthy saying that deserves full acceptance: Christ Jesus came into the world to save sinners — of whom I am the worst. But for that very reason I was shown mercy so that in me, the worst of sinners, Christ Jesus might display his unlimited patience as an example for those who would believe on him and receive eternal life."

1 Timothy 1:13-16

The person who believes that God loves him, as he is, with all of his "hang-ups," believes the unbelievable. Such love is beyond us, it's too good to be true. Now and then we catch a glimpse of it through the transformed lives of men like Sterling. Sometimes we see it reflected through the love of others. At still other times, it is just a feeling, a knowing that is too deep for words. And with the knowledge there comes a security, a confidence, that enables us to risk loving and living in ways we never dared before.

It seems to be that I understand God's love best when I've failed, fallen short of His grand design. Don't misunderstand me. I don't court failure, nor do I take pride in it. In fact, the longer I live for Jesus, the more painful failure becomes.

Sometimes it's something as ordinary as a broken relationship with all its misunderstanding and heartache. At other times it is simply the painful realization that I'm still not the person I hope to be, and with that realization comes an almost overwhelming sense of sinfulness. In the dark night of my soul I have cried out, "O Lord, will I ever be any different? Is there any hope for a man like me?"

In times like that, most of us are tempted to despair, to give up. Then we sense His love afresh. He hasn't forsaken us, hasn't given up on us. And once more we turn to Him and find Him turning to us.

Some years ago, I had an experience like that. Shame and love, guilt and grace all mixed together. In an attempt to sort out and make some sense of my feelings, I wrote in my journal:

196

"Sin has left me
feeling like a stranger,
 unknown and unknowing,
  unwelcome and unwanted.
Alienation and estrangement
are no longer just words,
but a painful reality which leaves me
wasted and wrung out.
I don't want to pray,
 I don't want to come into God's presence,
  I don't want to face Him.
I'm so ashamed,
 How could I be so sinful?
I'm afraid,
 Has He grown tired of my repeated failures,
  my constant confession?

"Still I come, for I cannot bear
 the pain and the burden of my sin alone.
My God, my God,
 why have You forsaken me?
You needn't answer.
I know my sin has driven me from You,
 broken our relationship,
  built a wall
   long and high.
I have no excuses,
 no self-justifying logic.
I cannot plead ignorance
 or extenuating circumstances.

"My self-inflicted punishment
 is more than I can bear.
My self-loathing is bitter bread
 which cannot ease the terrible hunger of my soul.
I pound upon the wall
 in frantic penitence,

until my fists are bruised and bloody,
    but it does not budge.
I try to scale the wall
    using the flimsy ladder
    of good works and self-righteousness,
    but my best efforts fail far short.

"Can You see me, Lord?
    Sitting here in the ever-deepening shadow
        of this imposing wall,
        bloody fists laying useless in my lap.
    Splintered pieces of broken ladder,
        scattered around me,
        in mute testimony
        to my futile efforts at reconciliation.

"The dirty rags of sinful failure
    cannot protect me from
    the cold night of despair.
I weep in my fear and guilt,
    my bruised lips give birth
    to broken sobs of confession,
    and the wall begins to tremble.
A stone moves,
    is shaken loose,
    and comes tumbling down with a frightful racket,
    then another and another,
    until there is a cross-shaped opening in the wall.

"A light shines through,
    embarrassing me,
    and I draw the rags of my shameful past
    about my naked soul.
In the light I see a nail-scarred hand,
    reaching out to me,
        bidding me come.
Fear and guilt mock me,
    and I withdraw involuntarily.

The shadows close about me,
    and my soul shivers.
The hand reaches into the darkness.
I want to grasp it,
    but to do so I must let go
    of the rags which hide my naked soul.
The conflict is almost debilitating.
    The hand promises
        light and warmth and fellowship,
            but my rags are familiar.
What if I drop them
    and reach for the hand,
        only to have Him turn away in revulsion?
The darkness grows deeper,
    closes around me like a casket,
    the cold cuts through my rags,
        and chills me with the touch of death.

"Dropping my filthy garments,
    I reach for the hand, grasp it,
        and He draws me toward the light.
Trembling, I step through
    the cross-shaped hole in the wall
        and emerge in the sunlight of His love.
For just a moment, I'm embarrassed
    and attempt to cover my nakedness
        only to discover that I'm clothed
        in the flowing garments of His forgiveness.

"There's a horrible sound,
    like the rumbling of an earthquake.
    I look behind me in time to see
    the wall come crashing down!
I can hardly believe my eyes.
    That impregnable wall,
    which absorbed my fiercest attacks without a dent,
    destroyed by a nail-scarred hand
    and a cross-shaped hole.

My eyes stare in hypnotic fascination
for several seconds more,
then His hand is upon my shoulder
and up ahead I hear the sound
of music and dancing.
Someone is shouting,
'The Father's son is found,
and He's throwing a party to celebrate.'
I turn to my Guide, my Savior, and ask,
'Am I invited?'
He replies,
'The celebration is in your honor.
You are His son!' "

At moments like that, we are overwhelmed. It seems our heart will burst, so full is it of love for God. As John the Beloved wrote, "We love him, because he first loved us" (1 John 4:19 KJV).

Then the most incredible thing begins to happen. God takes our love and turns it toward the loveless. Gently He speaks to our spirit: "My love is not to be paid back, but passed on."

Author Herbert Tarr describes an emotional parting which illustrates this truth as clearly as anything I know. He writes:

"The conductor called, 'All visitors off the train!' 'Oh, David...' She hugged him to her bosom which smelled of fruits and vegetables and a mother's love. 'Take care of him.' These last words were addressed not to Uncle Asher nor even to the conductor, but to God. Tante Dvorah spoke to Him freely and often, for the Lord, to her way of thinking, was a person-sitter to whom loved ones were safely entrusted, as well as her senior partner in the business of living, always accessible and invariably amenable to petitions of love.

"David looked at his aunt and uncle — she, with hands chapped and hard from selling fruit and vegetables outdoors in all kinds of weather, the face ruddy and round and invariably smiling, the heavy body more accustomed to a half a dozen sweaters at one time than a single coat, the hair the color of moonlight now, but the dark eyes still bright; he with his slight wiry body strong and bent from lifting too many fruit and vegetable crates for too many years, the wind-burned skin, the swarthy face impassive, except for the wry mouth — the childless couple who had taken the orphaned David into their home, rearing him since the age of seven yet refusing to be called 'Mama' and 'Papa' for fear that he would forget his real parents.

"David grabbed their rough peddlers' hands in his smooth student ones. 'How can I ever begin to pay you two for what you've done for me!' Uncle Asher spoke gently: 'David, there's a saying: "The love of parents goes to their children, but the love of these children goes to their children.' "

" 'That's not so!' David protested, 'I'll always be trying to —.' Tante Dvorah interrupted, 'David, what your uncle Asher means is that a parent's love isn't to be paid back; it can only be passed on.' "[11]

In moments like that, when I am especially aware of God's love, no task seems impossible, no distance too far, no cost too high, no sacrifice too great. I hear myself praying, "I'll pay You back, Lord, somehow, even if it takes my whole life." And when I'm especially sensitive to His nearness I hear Him say, "My love isn't to be paid back; it can only be passed on."

Most of the people we'll be required to love won't be very lovable, but that shouldn't really surprise us because we weren't very lovable either until we let Him love us. Even now we sometimes live and act in ways which would discourage any lover less determined than He. Perhaps this more than any one thing is what separates His holy love from the world's cheap counterfeits. He loves those who at first appear worthless and unlovable. And, miracle of miracles, He loves us into wholeness and makes us holy lovers too!

The world has now been infiltrated with these "holy lovers" carefully disguised as ordinary people. A few have captured the imagination of the world, howbeit not by design. There's the seventy-five-year-old Albanian nun named Teresa Bojaxhiu, better known to the world as Mother Theresa. In 1979 she won the Nobel Peace Prize.

Then there's Mark Buntain, a rather nondescript middle-aged man, a medical missionary, who built and directs the Calcutta Christian Mission Hospital in Calcutta, India. Every day, through his selfless love, thousands receive food, clothing and shelter, as well as medical treatment and a Christian witness.

And then there's "Grandma Howell," who at ninety-one was corresponding with seventeen prison inmates at one time. When she fell ill and it seemed she might die, one inmate pleaded in his childlike scrawl: "Please pray for Grandma Howell cause she's sick and may be going to die. *Nobody has ever loved me like she has.* I just wait for her letters, they means so much."[12] (emphasis mine)

Every weekend in the Bushwick section of Brooklyn, holy lovers, led by Bill Wilson, a visionary in blue jeans and jogging shoes, put their lives on the line to help ghetto kids find hope. Twenty yellow school buses bring almost 4000 children, mostly black and hispanic, to Sunday School which takes place in a converted beer brewery. There they take part in an enthusiastic service alive with music, singing, hand clapping, games, prizes and skits. It's fun of the purest kind, to be sure, but it is much more than that. They receive an evangelistic message about God's love, and they have an opportunity to receive Jesus Christ as their personal Savior. Hundreds are doing just that, and, as a result, they are escaping the drugs, crime and despair so automatic to many inner-city residents.

It's a dangerous ministry. Bill Wilson suffered his second heart attack at thirty-one, and he has been beaten and stabbed on more than one occasion. Other staffers have been mugged, and one worker in her twenties was savagely raped by three men on a rooftop. In addition to all of that, there is the constant financial pressure and the day to day desperation it brings. Still Bill Wilson and the Metro Assembly of God staff hang in there, loving those unlovable urchins with the love of God.

There are hundreds of thousands more, maybe millions. Men and women who have been touched and transformed by His holy love. "Blue-collar Christians" every one! The world will never take note of most of them, but eternity will reveal their redemptive work. Inconspicuously they go about the business of loving, not in their own strength, but in the power of His holy love. Some are missionaries serving in dangerously remote places, others are inner-city pastors. Some are professionals taking His love to the corporate offices situated high in the towering sanctuaries of business and finance. More often though, they are clerks and shopkeepers, social workers and housewives. Ordinary people living in extraordinary ways, bringing His holy love to a hurting world.

Dr. Victor G. Rosenblum is a professor of law and political science at Northwestern University, and the father of a retarded child whom he loves very much. He once was asked if he would favor permitting abortion if it were medically established that the baby was defective or would be retarded.

"Oh, no," he said, "no, no." Then he continued:

"Do you believe in love? I don't mean simple lip service to love. I am talking about life service. Do you really believe that we are here to love one another? If you do, then you don't say, 'I will love you because you have your mental faculties, and you because you are healthy, but not you because you have only one arm.' True love does not discriminate in this way.

"If we really believe in love, and find that a baby will be born having no arms, we would say, 'Baby, we are going to love you. We will make arms for you. We have many new skills now for doing this. And, Baby, if these arms don't work, we will be your arms. We will take care of you. You can be sure of that. You are one of us, a member of our human family, and we will always love you.' " (paraphrased)[13]

Love like that is rare indeed, but it's possible when we let God love us. And it is the heart and soul of Christianity. God becoming one of us, a man, showing us how to live and how to love. Dying on a cross, laying down His life in love for us and calling us to take His holy love to those who have never heard, who have never experienced His love. This is "blue-collar Christianity," a faith to die for! A faith to live for!

Footnotes:

1. William Barclay, *The Beatitudes and The Lord's Prayer for Everyman* (New York and Evanston: Harper & Row Publishers, 1968), pp. 69, 70.

2. Kathy C. Miller, *Out of Control* (Waco: Word Books Publisher), p. 114.

3. Miriam Neff, "As Near as Your Own Church Door" (*Moody*, May 1984), p. 20.

4. John Powell, S.J., *Abortion: the Silent Holocaust* (Allen: Argus Communications, 1981), p. 5.

5. Ibid.

6. Barclay, p. 68.

7. Ibid., p. 67.

8. Philip Yancey, *Helping Those In Pain* (*Leadership/84*, Spring Quarter), p. 91.

9. Ibid., p. 91.

10. Donald Macleod, *"Something Happened in Church," The Twentieth-Century Pulpit*, edited by James W. Cox (Nashville: Abingdon Press, 1978), p. 133.

11. Herbert Tarr, quoted in *Creative Brooding* by Robert Raines (New York: The Macmillan Company, 1966), p. 102.

12. Charles W. Colson, *Loving God* (Grand Rapids: A Judith Markham Book published by Zondervan Publishing House, 1983), p. 209.

13. Powell, p. 8.

BIBLIOGRAPHY

Anderson, Ann Kiemel and Ream, Jan Kiemel. *Struggling for Wholeness*. Nashville: Oliver-Nelson, 1986.

Barclay, William. *The Beatitudes and The Lord's Prayer for Everyman*. New York: Harper & Row, 1968.

Benson, Bob and Benson, Michael W. *Disciplines for the Inner Life*. Waco: Word Books, 1985.

Bergren, Wendy. "Mom Is Very Sick — Here's How to Help." Arcadia: Focus on the Family, 1982.

Britton, Janet. *Well, Janet Told Me. . . Moody*, January 1985.

Calkin, Ruth Harris. *Tell Me Again Lord, I Forget*. Elgin: David C. Cook, 1974.

Capote, Truman. *Music for Chameleons*. New York: Random House, 1980.

Claypool, John. *Tracks of a Fellow Struggler*. Waco: Word Books, 1974.

Collins, Gary R., Ph.D. *Christian Counseling*. Waco: Word Books, 1980.

Coloney, Joyce. "Confessions of a Happy Housewife." *Reader's Digest*, April 1982.

Colson, Charles. *Loving God*. Grand Rapids: Zondervan, 1983.

Craddock, Fred. "When the Roll Is Called Down Here." Preaching Today, Tape No. 50, 1987.

Dawnings, Finding God's Light in the Darkness. Edited by Phyllis Hobe. New York: Guideposts Associates, Inc., 1981.

Dunnam, Maxie. *Barefoot Days of the Soul*. Waco: Word Books.

Dunnam, Maxie. *The Communicator's Commentary Volume 8: Galatians, Ephesians, Philippians, Colossians, Philemon.* Waco: Word Books, 1982.

Elkins, Dov Peretz. *Glad to Be Me.* Englewood Cliffs: Prentice-Hall, 1976.

Exley, Richard. *The Painted Parable.* New York: Vantage Press, 1978.

Flint, Annie Johnson. "HE GIVETH MORE GRACE." Music by Hubert Mitchell. Lillenas Publishing Co., 1941, 1969.

Frankl, Victor. *Man's Search for Meaning.* New York: Pocket Books, 1963.

Galantly E. and Harris, B. *Marriage and Family Life.* Boston: Houghton Mifflin, 1982.

Gordon, Arthur. *A Touch of Wonder.* Old Tappan: Fleming H. Revell, 1984.

Gwaltney, John L. "Miz Mabel's Legacy." *Reader's Digest,* January 1982.

Hamilton, J. Wallace. *Where Now Is Thy God?* Old Tappan: Fleming H. Revell, 1969.

Hembree, Charles. *Pocket of Pebbles.* Grand Rapids: Baker Book House, 1969.

Hunter, Gordon C. *When the Walls Come Tumblin' Down.* Waco: Word Books, 1970.

Kiemel, Ann. *It's Incredible.* Wheaton: Tyndale House, 1977.

Kushner, Harold S. *When Bad Things Happen to Good People.* New York: Avon Books, 1981.

L'Engle, Madeleine. *Walking On Water.* Wheaton: Harold Shaw, 1980.

Littauer, Florence. *Lives on the Mend.* Waco: Word Books, 1985.

Miller, Kathy. *Out of Control.* Waco: Word Books.

"My Husband Left Me For A Younger Woman." *Good Housekeeping,* October 1983.

Neff, Miriam. "As Near as Your Own Church Door." *Moody,* May 1984.

Porter, Katherine Anne. *Ship of Fools.* Boston: Little, Brown & Co., 1962.

Powell, John, S.J. *Abortion: the Silent Holocaust.* Allen: Argus Communications, 1981.

Raines, Robert. *Creative Brooding.* New York: Macmillan, 1966.

Smith, Fred. *You and Your Network.* Waco: Word Books, 1984.

Stewart, James S. *The Wind of the Spirit*. Nashville: Abingdon, 1968.

The Twentieth Century Pulpit. Edited by James W. Cox. Nashville: Abingdon, 1978.

Wangerin, Walter Jr. *As For Me And My House*. Nashville: Thomas Nelson, 1987.

Welter, Paul R., Ed.D. *Counseling and the Search for Meaning*. Waco: Word Books, 1987.

Wright, H. Norman. *Training Christians to Counsel*. Denver: Christian Marriage Enrichment.

Yancey, Philip. *Helping Those In Pain*. *Leadership/84*, Spring Quarter.

To Pam + J who —

May you always have the joy
of being in "the cello," darling.

We love and appreciate you.

[signature]